The Power
of Full
Engagement

The Power
of Full
Engagement

Managing Energy, Not Time,
Is the Key to High Performance
and Personal Renewal

Jim Loehr and Tony Schwartz

LARGE PRINT

This large print edition published in 2003 by
RB Large Print
A division of Recorded Books
A Haights Cross Communications Company
270 Skipjack Road
Prince Frederick, MD 20678

First published by The Free Press, a division of
Simon & Schuster, 2003

Publisher's Cataloging In Publication Data
(Prepared by Donohue Group, Inc.)

Loehr, Jim.
   The power of full engagement : managing energy, not time, is
the key to high performance and personal renewal / Jim Loehr
and Tony Schwartz.

   p. ; cm.

   Includes bibliographical references.
   ISBN: 1–4025–5838–4

1. Success—Psychological aspects. 2. Large type books.
I. Schwartz, Tony II. Title.

BF637.S8 L573 2003b
158.1

Typeset by Palimpsest Book Production Limited,
Polmont, Stirlingshire, Scotland
Printed in the United States of America
By Bang Printing
3323 Oak Street
Brainerd, Minnesota 56401

To Our Parents
Con & Mary
Felice & Irving

CONTENTS

PART ONE

THE DYNAMICS
OF
FULL ENGAGEMENT

CHAPTER 1

FULLY ENGAGED:
ENERGY, NOT TIME,
IS OUR MOST PRECIOUS
RESOURCE

We live in digital time. Our rhythms are rushed, rapid fire and relentless, our days carved up into bits and bytes. We celebrate breadth rather than depth, quick reaction more than considered reflection. We skim across the surface, alighting for brief moments at dozens of destinations but rarely remaining for long at any one. We race through our lives without pausing to consider who we really want to be or where we really want to go. We're wired up but we're melting down.

Most of us are just trying to do the best that we can. When demand exceeds our capacity, we begin to make expedient choices that get us through our days and nights, but take a toll over time. We survive on too little sleep, wolf down fast foods on the run, fuel up with coffee and cool down with alcohol and sleeping pills. Faced with relentless demands at work, we become short-tempered and easily distracted. We return home from long days at work feeling exhausted and often experience our families not as a source of joy and renewal, but as one more demand in an already overburdened life.

We walk around with day planners and to-do lists, Palm Pilots and BlackBerries, instant pagers and pop-up reminders on our computers—all designed to help us manage our time better. We take pride in our ability to multitask, and we wear our willingness to put in long hours as a badge of honor. The term 24/7 describes a world in which work never ends. We use words like obsessed, crazed and overwhelmed not to describe insanity, but instead to characterize our everyday lives. Feeling forever starved for time, we assume that we have no choice but to cram as much as possible into every day. But managing time efficiently is no guarantee that we will bring sufficient energy to whatever it is we are doing.

Consider these scenarios:

- You attend a four-hour meeting in which not a single second is wasted—but during the final two hours your energy level drops off precipitously and you struggle to stay focused.
- You race through a meticulously scheduled twelve-hour day but by midday your energy has turned negative—impatient, edgy and irritable.

4

- You set aside time to be with your children when you get home at the end of the day, but you are so distracted by thoughts about work that you never really give them your full attention.
- You remember your spouse's birthday—your computer alerts you and so does your Palm Pilot—but by the evening, you are too tired to go out and celebrate.

**Energy, not time,
is the fundamental currency
of high performance.**

This insight has revolutionized our thinking about what drives enduring high performance. It has also prompted dramatic transformations in the way our clients manage their lives, personally and professionally. Everything they do—from interacting with colleagues and making important decisions to spending time with their families—requires energy. Obvious as this seems, we often fail to take into account the importance of energy at work and in our personal lives. Without the right quantity, quality, focus and force of energy, we are compromised in any activity we undertake.

Every one of our thoughts, emotions and behaviors has an energy consequence, for better or for worse. The ultimate measure of our lives is not how much time we spend on the planet, but rather how much energy we invest in the time that we have. The premise of this book—and of the training we do each year with thousands of clients—is simple enough:

**Performance, health and happiness
are grounded in the
skillful management of energy.**

There are undeniably bad bosses, toxic work environments, difficult relationships and real life crises. Nonetheless, we have far more control over our energy than we ordinarily realize. The number of hours in a day is fixed, but the quantity and quality of energy available to us is not. It is our most precious resource. The more we take responsibility for the energy we bring to the world, the more empowered and productive we become. The more we blame others or external circumstances, the more negative and compromised our energy is likely to be.

If you could wake up tomorrow with significantly more positive, focused energy to invest at work and with your family, how significantly would that change your life for the better? As a leader and a manager, how valuable would it be to bring more positive energy and passion to the workplace? If those you lead could call on more positive energy, how would it affect their relationships with one another, and the quality of service that they deliver to customers and clients?

Leaders are the stewards of organizational energy—in companies, organizations and even in

6

families. They inspire or demoralize others first by how effectively they manage their own energy and next by how well they mobilize, focus, invest and renew the collective energy of those they lead. The skillful management of energy, individually and organizationally, makes possible something that we call full engagement.

To be fully engaged, we must be physically energized, emotionally connected, mentally focused and spiritually aligned with a purpose beyond our immediate self-interest. Full engagement begins with feeling eager to get to work in the morning, equally happy to return home in the evening and capable of setting clear boundaries between the two. It means being able to immerse yourself in the mission you are on, whether that is grappling with a creative challenge at work, managing a group of people on a project, spending time with loved ones or simply having fun. Full engagement implies a fundamental shift in the way we live our lives.

Less than 30 percent of American workers are fully engaged at work, according to data collected by the Gallup Organization in early 2001. Some 55 percent are "not engaged." Another 19 percent are "actively disengaged," meaning not just that they are unhappy at work, but that they regularly share those feelings with colleagues. The costs of a disengaged workforce run into the trillions of dollars. Worse yet, the longer employees stay with organizations, the less engaged they become. Gallup found that after six months on the job,

THE POWER OF FULL ENGAGEMENT

Old Paradigm	New Paradigm
Manage time	Manage energy
Avoid stress	Seek stress
Life is a marathon	Life is a series of sprints
Downtime is wasted time	Downtime is productive time
Rewards fuel performance	Purpose fuels performance
Self-discipline rules	Rituals rule
The power of positive thinking	The power of full engagement

only 38 percent of employees remain engaged. After three years, the figure drops to 22 percent. Think about your own life. How fully engaged are you at work? What about your colleagues or the people who work for you?

During the past decade, we have grown increasingly disturbed by the myriad ways in which our clients squander and misuse their energy. These include everything from poor eating habits and failure to seek regular recovery and renewal to negativity and poor focus. The lessons we seek to impart in this book have proved to be profoundly useful in managing our own lives and in leading our own organization. When we follow the energy management principles and the change process that we share on these pages, we find that we are far more effective, both personally and professionally, in our own actions and in our relationships. When we fall short, we see the costs immediately, in our performance and in our impact on others. The same is true of tens of thousands of clients with whom we have worked. Learning to manage energy more efficiently and intelligently has a unique transformative power, both individually and organizationally.

A LIVING LABORATORY

We first learned about the importance of energy in the living laboratory of professional sports. For thirty years, our organization has worked with world-class athletes, defining precisely what it takes to perform consistently at the highest levels under intense competitive pressures. Our initial clients were tennis players. Over eighty of the world's best players have been through our laboratory, among them Pete Sampras, Jim Courier, Arantxa Sanchez-Vicario, Tom and Tim Gullikson, Sergi Bruguera, Gabriela Sabatini and Monica Seles.

These players typically came to us when they were struggling, and our interventions have often produced dramatic turnarounds. After we worked with them, Sanchez-Vicario won the U.S. Open for the first time and became the top-ranked player in the world in both singles and doubles, and Sabatini won her first and only U.S. Open title. Bruguera went from number 79 in the world to the top ten and won two French Open titles. We went on to train a broad range of professional athletes, among them golfers Mark O'Meara and Ernie Els; hockey players Eric Lindros and Mike Richter; boxer Ray "Boom Boom" Mancini; basketball players Nick Anderson and Grant Hill; and speed skater Dan Jansen, who won his only Olympic gold medal following two intensive years of training with us.

What makes our intervention with athletes unique is that we spend no time focusing on their technical or tactical skills. Conventional wisdom holds that if you find talented people and equip them with the right skills for the challenge at hand, they will perform at their best. In our experience that often isn't so. Energy is the X factor that makes it possible to fully ignite talent and skill. We never addressed how Monica Seles hit her serves, or how Mark O'Meara drove the ball, or how Grant Hill shot his free throws. All of these athletes were extraordinarily gifted and accomplished when they came to us. We focused instead on helping them to manage their energy more effectively in the service of whatever mission they were on.

Athletes turned out to be a demanding experimental group. They aren't satisfied with inspirational messages or clever theories about performance. They seek measurable, enduring results. They care about batting averages, free-throw percentages, tournament victories and year-end rankings. They want to be able to sink the putt on the eighteenth hole in the final round, hit the free throw when the game is on the line, catch the pass in a crowd with a minute to go on the clock. Anything else is just talk. If we couldn't deliver results for athletes, we didn't last very long in their lives. We learned to be accountable to the numbers.

As word spread about our success in sports, we received numerous requests to export our model into other high-performance venues. We began working with FBI hostage rescue teams, U.S. marshals, and critical-care workers in hospitals. Today, the bulk of our work is in business—with executives and entrepreneurs, managers and sales people, and more recently with teachers and clergy, lawyers and medical students. Our corporate clients include Fortune 500 companies such as Estée Lauder, Salomon Smith Barney, Pfizer, Merrill Lynch, Bristol-Myers Squibb, and the Hyatt Corporation.

Along the way, we discovered something completely unexpected: The performance demands that most people face in their everyday work environments dwarf those of any professional athletes we have ever trained.

How is that possible?

It's not as anomalous as it seems. Professional athletes typically spend about 90 percent of their time training, in order to be able to perform 10 percent of the time. Their entire lives are designed around expanding, sustaining and renewing the energy they need to compete for short, focused periods of time. At a practical level, they build very precise routines for managing energy in all spheres of their lives—eating and sleeping; working out and resting; summoning the appropriate emotions; mentally preparing and staying focused; and connecting regularly to the mission they have set for themselves. Although most of us spend little or no time systematically training in any of these dimensions, we are expected to perform at our best for eight, ten and even twelve hours a day.

Most professional athletes also enjoy an off-season of four to five months a year. After competing under extraordinary pressure for several months, a long off-season gives athletes the critical time that they need for rest and healing, renewal and growth. By contrast, your "off season" likely amounts to a few weeks of vacation a year. Even then, you probably aren't solely resting and recovering. More likely, you are spending at least some of your vacation time answering email, checking your voice mail and ruminating about your work.

Finally, professional athletes have an average

career span of five to seven years. If they have handled their finances reasonably well, they are often set for life. Few of them are under pressure to run out and get another job. By contrast, you can probably expect to work for forty to fifty years without any significant breaks.

Given these stark facts, what makes it possible to keep performing at your best without sacrificing your health, your happiness and your passion for life?

You must become a Corporate Athlete.®

The challenge of great performance is to manage your energy more effectively in all dimensions to achieve your goals. Four key energy management principles drive this process. They lie at the heart of the change process that we will describe in the pages ahead, and they are critical for building the capacity to live a productive, fully engaged life.

PRINCIPLE 1:

Full engagement requires drawing on four
separate but related sources of energy:
physical, emotional, mental and spiritual.

Human beings are complex energy systems, and full engagement is not simply one-dimensional. The energy that pulses through us is physical, emotional, mental, and spiritual. All four dynamics are critical, none is sufficient by itself and each profoundly influences the others. To perform at our best, we must skillfully manage each of these interconnected dimensions of energy. Subtract any one from the equation and our capacity to fully ignite our talent and skill is diminished, much the way an engine sputters when one of its cylinders misfires.

Energy is the common denominator in all dimensions of our lives. Physical energy capacity is measured in terms of quantity (low to high) and emotional capacity in quality (negative to positive). These are our most fundamental sources of energy because without sufficient high-octane

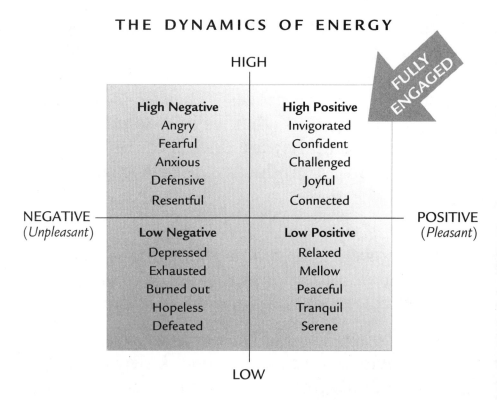

THE DYNAMICS OF ENERGY

fuel no mission can be accomplished. The accompanying chart depicts the dynamics of energy from low to high and from negative to positive. The more toxic and unpleasant the energy, the less effectively it serves performance; the more positive and pleasant the energy, the more efficient it is. Full engagement and maximum performance are possible only in the high positive quadrant.

The importance of full engagement is most vivid in situations where the consequences of disengagement are profound. Imagine for a moment that you are facing open-heart surgery. Which energy quadrant do you want your surgeon to be in? How would you feel if he entered the operating room feeling angry, frustrated and anxious (high negative)? How about overworked, exhausted and depressed (low negative)? What if he was disengaged, laid back and slightly spacey (low positive)? Obviously, you want your surgeon energized, confident and upbeat (high positive).

Imagine that every time you yelled at someone in frustration or did sloppy work on a project or failed to focus your attention fully on the task at hand, you put someone's life at risk. Very quickly, you would become less negative, reckless and sloppy in the way you manage your energy. We hold ourselves accountable for the ways that we manage our time, and for that matter our money. We must learn to hold ourselves at least equally accountable for how we manage our energy physically, emotionally, mentally and spiritually.

PRINCIPLE 2:

Because energy capacity diminishes both with overuse and with underuse, we must balance energy expenditure with intermittent energy renewal.

We rarely consider how much energy we are spending because we take it for granted that the

THE MIND AND BODY ARE ONE

The primary markers of physical capacity are strength, endurance, flexibility and resilience. These are precisely the same markers of capacity emotionally, mentally and spiritually. Flexibility at the physical level, for example, means that the muscle has a broad range of motion. Stretching increases flexibility.

The same is true emotionally. Emotional flexibility reflects the capacity to move freely and appropriately along a wide spectrum of emotions rather than responding rigidly or defensively. Emotional resilience is the ability to bounce back from experiences of disappointment, frustration and even loss.

Mental endurance is a measure of the ability to sustain focus and concentration over time, while mental flexibility is marked by the capacity to move between the rational and the intuitive and to embrace multiple points of view.

16

Spiritual strength is reflected in the commitment to one's deepest values, regardless of circumstance and even when adhering to them involves personal sacrifice. Spiritual flexibility, by contrast, reflects the tolerance for values and beliefs that are different than one's own, so long as those values and beliefs don't bring harm to others.

In short, to be fully engaged requires strength, endurance, flexibility and resilience in all dimensions.

energy available to us is limitless. In fact, increased demand progressively depletes our energy reserves—especially in the absence of any effort to reverse the progressive loss of capacity that occurs with age. By training in all dimensions we can dramatically slow our decline physically and mentally, and we can actually deepen our emotional and spiritual capacity until the very end of our lives.

By contrast, when we live highly linear lives—spending far more energy than we recover or recovering more than we spend—the eventual consequence is that we break down, burn out, atrophy, lose our passion, get sick and even die prematurely. Sadly, the need for recovery is often viewed as evidence of weakness rather than as an integral aspect of sustained performance. The result is that we give almost no attention to renewing and expanding our energy reserves, individually or organizationally.

**To maintain a powerful pulse
in our lives, we must learn
how to rhythmically spend
and renew energy.**

The richest, happiest and most productive lives are characterized by the ability to fully engage in the challenge at hand, but also to disengage periodically and seek renewal. Instead, many of us live our lives as if we are running in an endless marathon, pushing ourselves far beyond healthy levels of exertion. We become flat liners mentally and emotionally by relentlessly spending energy without sufficient recovery. We become flat liners physically and spiritually by not expending enough energy. Either way, we slowly but inexorably wear down.

Think for a moment about the look of many long-distance runners: gaunt, sallow, slightly sunken and emotionally flat. Now visualize a sprinter such as Marion Jones or Michael Johnson. Sprinters typically look powerful, bursting with energy and eager to push themselves to their limits. The explanation is simple. No matter how intense the demand they face, the finish line is clearly visible 100 or 200 meters down the track. We, too, must learn to live our own lives as a series of sprints—fully engaging for periods of time, and then fully disengaging and seeking renewal before jumping back into the fray to face whatever challenges confront us.

PRINCIPLE 3:

To build capacity, we must push beyond
our normal limits, training in the same
systematic way that elite athletes do.

Stress is not the enemy in our lives. Paradoxically, it is the key to growth. In order to build strength in a muscle we must systematically stress it, expending energy beyond normal levels. Doing so literally causes microscopic tears in the muscle fibers. At the end of a training session, functional capacity is diminished. But give the muscle twenty-four to forty-eight hours to recover and it grows stronger and better able to handle the next stimulus. While this training phenomenon has been applied largely to building physical strength, it is just as relevant to building "muscles" in every dimension of our lives—from empathy and patience to focus and creativity to integrity and commitment. What applies to the body applies equally to the other dimensions of our lives. This insight both simplifies and revolutionizes the way we approach the barriers that stand in our way.

**We build emotional,
mental and spiritual capacity
in precisely the same way
that we build physical capacity.**

We grow at all levels by expending energy beyond our ordinary limits and then recovering. Expose a muscle to ordinary demand and it won't grow. With age it will actually lose strength. The limiting factor in building any "muscle" is that many of us back off at the slightest hint of discomfort. To meet increased demand in our lives, we must learn to systematically build and strengthen muscles wherever our capacity is insufficient. Any form of stress that prompts discomfort has the potential to expand our capacity—physically, mentally, emotionally or spiritually—so long as it is followed by adequate recovery. As Nietzsche put it, "That which does not kill us makes us stronger." Because the demands on Corporate Athletes are greater and more enduring than those on professional athletes, it is even more critical that they learn to train systematically.

PRINCIPLE 4:

Positive energy rituals—highly specific routines for managing energy—are the key to full engagement and sustained high performance.

Change is difficult. We are creatures of habit. Most of what we do is automatic and nonconscious.

What we did yesterday is what we are likely to do today. The problem with most efforts at change is that conscious effort can't be sustained over the long haul. Will and discipline are far more limited resources than most of us realize. If you have to think about something each time you do it, the likelihood is that you won't keep doing it for very long. The status quo has a magnetic pull on us.

A positive ritual is a behavior that becomes automatic over time—fueled by some deeply held value.

We use the word "ritual" purposefully to empha-size the notion of a carefully defined, highly struc-tured behavior. In contrast to will and discipline, which require pushing yourself to a particular behavior, a ritual pulls at you. Think of something as simple as brushing your teeth. It is not some-thing that you ordinarily have to remind yourself to do. Brushing your teeth is something to which you feel consistently drawn, compelled by its clear health value. You do it largely on automatic pilot, without much conscious effort or intention. The power of rituals is that they insure that we use as little conscious energy as possible where it is not absolutely necessary, leaving us free to strategi-cally focus the energy available to us in creative, enriching ways.

Look at any part of your life in which you are

consistently effective and you will find that certain habits help make that possible. If you eat in a healthy way, it is probably because you have built routines around the food you buy and what you are willing to order at restaurants. If you are fit, it is probably because you have regular days and times for working out. If you are successful in a sales job, you probably have a ritual of mental preparation for calls and ways that you talk to yourself to stay positive in the face of rejection. If you manage others effectively, you likely have a style of giving feedback that leaves people feeling challenged rather than threatened. If you are closely connected to your spouse and your children, you probably have rituals around spending time with them. If you sustain high positive energy despite an extremely demanding job, you almost certainly have predictable ways of insuring that you get intermittent recovery. Creating positive rituals is the most powerful means we have found to effectively manage energy in the service of full engagement.

THE CHANGE PROCESS

Making all of this happen is another story. How can we build and sustain the multidimensional energy that we need—particularly as the demands in our lives intensify and our capacity diminishes inexorably with age?

Making changes that endure, we have found, is

a three-step process that we call Purpose-Truth-Action. All three are necessary and none is sufficient by itself.

The first step in our change process is to Define Purpose. In the face of our habitual behaviors and our instinct to preserve the status quo, we need inspiration to make changes in our lives. Our first challenge is to answer the question "How should I spend my energy in a way that is consistent with my deepest values?" The consequence of living our lives at warp speed is that we rarely take the time to reflect on what we value most deeply or to keep these priorities front and center. Most of us spend more time reacting to immediate crises and responding to the expectations of others than we do making considered choices guided by a clear sense of what matters most.

In the purpose stage, our goal is to help clients to surface and articulate the most important values in their lives and to define a vision for themselves, both personally and professionally. Connecting to a deep set of values and creating a compelling vision fuels a uniquely high-octane source of energy for change. It also serves as a compass for navigating the storms that inevitably arise in our lives.

It is impossible to chart a course of change until you are able to look honestly at who you are today. In the next stage of our process, Face the Truth, the first question we ask clients is "How are you spending your energy now?" Each of us finds ways

23

to avoid the most unpleasant and discomfiting truths in our lives. We regularly underestimate the consequences of our energy management choices, failing to honestly acknowledge the foods we are eating; how much alcohol we are consuming; what quality of energy we are investing in our relationships with our bosses, colleagues, spouses and children; and how focused and passionate we really are at work. Too often, we view our lives through rose-colored glasses, painting ourselves as victims, or simply denying to ourselves that the choices we are making are having a consequential impact on the quantity, quality, force and focus of our energy.

Facing the truth begins with gathering credible data. When clients come to us, we take them through a variety of physical tests, carefully assess their diets, and give them a detailed questionnaire designed to measure precisely how they are managing their energy physically, emotionally, mentally and spiritually. We also have five of their closest colleagues fill out a similar questionnaire. All of this data give us a clear picture of their current energy capacity and the obstacles that stand in the way of full engagement.

To launch this process for yourself, we encourage you to take a first step. Log on to our PowerofFullEngagement.com website and take a brief version of our Full Engagement Inventory. The scores that you receive will provide baseline data about your primary performance barriers. For a more detailed analysis of how you are managing your energy emotionally, physically and spiritually, you can arrange to take our complete Full Engagement Inventory online. For either test, you will be asked to have five other people in your life—or as close to five as you can get—anonymously fill out a similar set of questions about you. Facing the truth requires gathering as much comprehensive and objective data as is possible.

The third step in your change process is to Take Action to close the gap between who you are and who you want to be—between how you manage your energy now and how you want to manage your energy to achieve whatever mission you are on. This step involves building a personal-development plan grounded in positive energy rituals. Some of our existing habits serve us well, but others are more expedient. They help us get through the day, but take a long-term toll on our performance, health and happiness. Examples include relying on junk food for bursts of energy; smoking or drinking to manage anxiety; furiously multitasking to meet demands; setting aside more challenging, long-term projects in favor of what feels immediately pressing and easier to accomplish, and devoting little energy to personal relationships. The costs of these choices and many others only show up over time.

But just as negative habits and routines in our lives can be undermining and destructive, so positive ones can be uplifting and revitalizing. It is possible to build and sustain energy in all dimensions of our lives rather than watching passively as our capacities slowly diminish with age. Building rituals requires defining very precise behaviors and performing them at very specific times—motivated by deeply held values. As Aristotle said: "We are what we repeatedly do." Or as the Dalai Lama put it more recently: "There isn't anything that isn't made easier through constant familiarity and training. Through training we can change; we can transform ourselves."

The story of Roger B., one of our clients, vividly demonstrates how the casual choices that we make each day, often without thinking much about them, can slowly lead to compromised energy, diminished performance and a progressively disengaged life. In the chapters that follow, we lay out both a model and a systematic program by which to better mobilize, manage, focus and regularly renew your energy—and the energy of others. This training process ultimately proved to be transformative for Roger B. It has been highly effective for thousands of others and we hope it will be just as life changing for you.

BEAR IN MIND

- Managing energy, not time, is the fundamental currency of high performance. Performance is grounded in the skillful management of energy.
- Great leaders are stewards of organizational energy. They begin by effectively managing their

own energy. As leaders, they must mobilize, focus, invest, channel, renew and expand the energy of others.

- Full engagement is the energy state that best serves performance.
- Principle 1: Full engagement requires drawing on four separate but related sources of energy: physical, emotional, mental and spiritual.
- Principle 2: Because energy diminishes both with overuse and with underuse, we must balance energy expenditure with intermittent energy renewal.
- Principle 3: To build capacity we must push beyond our normal limits, training in the same systematic way that elite athletes do.
- Principle 4: Positive energy rituals—highly specific routines for managing energy—are the key to full engagement and sustained high performance.
- Making change that lasts requires a three-step process: Define Purpose, Face the Truth and Take Action.

CHAPTER 2

THE DISENGAGED LIFE
OF ROGER B.

When he came to work with us at our training facility in Orlando, Florida, Roger B. seemed to be living a quintessentially successful life. At forty-two, he was a sales manager for a large software company. He had a six-figure salary, responsibility over four western states, and eighteen months earlier he had been named a vice president, his fourth promotion in less than six years. He met his wife Rachel, thirty-nine, in college, and they began dating in their mid-twenties. Married for fifteen years, they had two children—nine-year-old Alyssa and seven-year-old Isabel—and Rachel had her own busy career as a school psychologist. They lived in a suburb of Phoenix, on a cul-de-sac with a half dozen other young families, in a house that they had helped to design themselves. Between their demanding careers and the challenge of raising two kids who had busy schedules of their own, life was very full. But it was also a life that they had worked hard to achieve. At first blush, it was difficult to see much of a problem.

Nonetheless, when Roger came to see us, we knew that his boss was increasingly unhappy with his performance at work. "We considered Roger a rising star for many years," his boss had told us. "I really don't know what happened. Two years ago, we gave him a big promotion into an important leadership position, and since then he's gone from an A-level performer to a C plus at best. It's affecting his whole sales force. I'm disappointed and frustrated. I haven't completely given up hope, but if something doesn't change soon, he's not going to make it. Nothing would make me happier than if you could help him get back on track. He's a good man with a lot of talent. I would hate to have to let him go."

A critical part of our process involves taking a closer look at what is going on beneath the surface of our clients' lives. Facing the Truth begins with our Full Engagement Inventory—a highly detailed questionnaire designed to surface people's behavioral patterns and to measure how effectively they are spending and recovering energy in all dimensions of their lives. In addition, Roger filled out a brief medical history and a comprehensive nutritional profile, detailing precisely what he had eaten on three designated days. When he got to our facility, we put him through a number of physical tests, which included assessing his cardiovascular capacity, strength, flexibility, body fat percentage and blood chemistry markers such as his cholesterol level. Obviously it isn't possible to get the same physical data by reading this book, but if you aren't doing the sort of regular cardiovascular and strength training recommended in chapter 3, you are almost certainly progressively losing energy capacity.

Roger's data indicated five primary performance barriers: low energy, impatience, negativity, lack of depth in relationships, and lack of passion. While he found it disturbing to receive this feedback from colleagues, his self-assessment was only slightly more positive. All performance barriers, we have found, are attributable to poor energy management—either in the form of insufficient energy renewal, insufficient energy capacity or, more typically, both. In addition, any given performance barrier is almost always influenced by multidimensional factors.

PHYSICAL IS FUNDAMENTAL

In Roger's case, the most obvious contributing factor in all of his performance barriers was the way that he managed his physical energy. All through high school and college, he had been an athlete. He played basketball and tennis and prided himself on being in excellent shape. On his medical form, he rated himself as five to ten pounds overweight, but in answer to another question, he acknowledged that he had gained twenty-three pounds since graduating from high school. His body fat percentage was 27—average for the male clients that we see, but more than 25 percent over the acceptable limit for a man his age. His belly now peeked out over his belt, a sign of middle age that he had always sworn would never happen to him.

At his latest checkup, Roger's blood pressure had been measured at 150 over 90, just on the cusp of hypertensive. He acknowledged that his physician had urged him to make some changes in his diet, and to get more exercise. His total cholesterol level was 235—significantly above the ideal level. Roger had quit smoking a decade earlier, although he confessed that he still had an occasional cigarette when he felt especially stressed. "I don't consider that smoking," he said, "and I don't want to talk about it."

Roger's eating habits went a long way toward explaining his weight gain and his problems with low energy. Most days, he skipped breakfast altogether ("I'm always trying to lose weight"), but he frequently broke down at midmorning and ordered a blueberry muffin with his second cup of coffee. When he was in the office, he usually consumed lunch at his desk, and while he tried hard to limit himself to a sandwich and a salad, he frequently also had a large bowl of frozen yogurt for dessert. When he was traveling, he often just grabbed a hamburger and fries for lunch, or a couple of slices of pizza on the run.

Around 4:00 p.m. on most days, his energy flagging badly, Roger often treated himself to a handful of cookies, which always seemed to be around the office. Over the course of a day his energy spiked and crashed, depending on how long he had gone without eating and what sort of sugary snacks he ate. The energy crashes strongly influenced both his level of irritability and his capacity for focus. Dinner was Roger's biggest meal and the primary factor in his weight gain. By the time that he sat down at 7:30 or 8:00 p.m., he was usually famished and ready for something substantial—a big bowl of pasta or a generous portion of chicken or steak, potatoes, a well-dressed salad and lots of bread. About half the time he managed to resist eating another sugary snack before bed.

Roger nearly always managed to resist exercise, which would have offset some of the effects of overeating and also provided a powerful way to detoxify negative emotions and to renew mentally. His explanation was that he simply couldn't find the time or the energy to work out. He was on the road most mornings at 6:30. By the time he got home in the evenings, beat from an hour-and-fifteen-minute commute, the last thing he wanted to do was take a jog, or jump on the stationary bike in his basement. Instead it sat unused alongside other earlier inspirations—a rowing machine, a Nordic track and a hulking pile of free weights.

The previous Christmas, Rachel had bought Roger a membership in the health club near his office and several sessions with a personal trainer. The first week he went three times and started to feel that he was on a roll. The second week he got there only once. Within a month, he had quit going altogether. During the warm weather, Roger played golf on most Saturdays, and while he wouldn't have minded walking the course, his partners preferred riding in the cart. He tried to get out for a brisk walk on Sunday mornings, but family obligations often got in the way. The result had been a progressive drop in his endurance over the years. At this stage in Roger's life, climbing two flights of stairs when the elevator in his office was out of order left him feeling winded—and embarrassed.

To unwind from the stresses of the day, Roger typically had a martini when he got home at night and a glass or two of wine with dinner, which only made him more tired. Even so, he found it hard to get himself to bed at a reasonable hour, and when he finally turned out the light around 12:30 or 1:00 a.m., after taking one last check of his email, he often slept fitfully, and at most for five to six hours. At least once or twice a week, the struggle to fall asleep reached the point that he took a sleeping pill.

On the nights he entertained clients, Roger acknowledged that he often had more to drink.

Dinners started and ended later, and the wine usually flowed freely. Between a cocktail reception and a long dinner, it wasn't uncommon to consume three or four glasses of wine in the course of an evening. Not only did that add several hundred empty calories to his diet, it also frequently left him feeling groggy the next morning.

Without caffeine, Roger would have had a hard time getting through his days. He tried to limit himself to two cups of coffee in the morning—three on a day when he really felt exhausted. He had twice tried to quit coffee, but when he did, he got terrible headaches. By keeping a nutritional log before coming to visit us, Roger also discovered that he was adding to his caffeine intake by consuming two or three diet colas each afternoon. Cumulatively, Roger's choices took a severe toll not only on the quantity and quality of energy available to him, but also on his focus and his motivation.

RUNNING ON EMPTY

At the emotional level, Roger's primary performance barriers were impatience and negativity. He found this sobering. Just as he had grown up thinking of himself as an athlete, so Roger had always considered himself easygoing. In high school, and in his fraternity at college, he was known as friendly and funny, the guy you could always count on for a good time. At the office in his early years, he was the person who made everyone in the office laugh. Over time, however, his humor had acquired an edge. Where it had once been mostly gentle and self-deprecating, now it was often sarcastic and edgy.

Low energy was plainly a factor since it made Roger more vulnerable to negative emotions. At the same time, there was little about his current life that made him feel positive. During Roger's first seven years at his company, the pressures were high, but the opportunities were great. His boss was a nurturing man who mentored him, liked his ideas, gave him lots of freedom and helped him to advance rapidly up the corporate ladder. His boss's positive energy made Roger feel better about himself.

Now the company was experiencing a slowdown, expenses were being cut, layoffs had begun and everyone was expected to do more with less. His boss had been given broader responsibilities, Roger saw much less of him, and he couldn't help but feel that he had fallen out of favor. It affected not just his mood, but also his passion for his work, and ultimately his performance. Energy is highly infectious, and negativity feeds on itself. Leaders have a disproportionate impact on the energy of others. Roger's moods powerfully influenced those who worked for him, much as the feeling of being neglected by his own boss deeply affected Roger's energy.

Relationships are one of the most powerful potential sources of emotional renewal. For years, Roger had thought of Rachel as both his lover and his best friend. Now, with so little time together, the feeling of romance and intimacy seemed like a distant memory and sex had become much less frequent. Their relationship was increasingly transactional. Conversations focused largely on household logistics and negotiations—who was going to pick up the dry cleaning or the takeout dinner, which kid needed a ride to which after-school activity. They spent very little time talking with each other about what was really going on in their lives.

Rachel had her own preoccupations. Her job as a psychologist covering several schools was demanding in itself. A year earlier, her father had been diagnosed with Alzheimer's at the age of seventy-seven and his deterioration was rapid. What little time Rachel previously had for herself—particularly for working out, which she craved as a way to keep her weight down and to relieve tension—was now gone. Instead, she spent much of her free time helping her mother with the increasingly demanding task of caring for her father. The pressure of her father's illness, added to the demands of being a mother and working at a full-time job, had plainly sapped her energy reserves. It also made her even less available to Roger. He understood the stresses that Rachel was under, but couldn't help feeling a bit abandoned, much as he did by his boss.

Meanwhile, Alyssa, nine, had begun having some problems in school. After testing, it turned out that she had some modest learning disabilities. She became convinced that she was "stupid," and it was beginning to affect her schoolwork and her social life. Roger knew that Alyssa needed attention and reassurance, but often he just couldn't summon the energy to reach out to her in the evenings. Isabel, the seven-year-old, seemed to be doing fine, but Roger's fatigue also affected his relationship with her. When she sought him out to play cards or Monopoly with her, he often begged off or suggested that they watch television together instead.

As for friendship, there just wasn't much time, given all the other demands in his life. The three friends that Roger did see regularly were his golfing buddies, and while he found the time they spent together relaxing, it wasn't especially satisfying. Competing noisily on the golf course and then smoking cigars and drinking beer in the clubhouse afterward felt more like fraternity life than real friendship. Rachel didn't have much use for the guys and resented the time that Roger spent playing golf. He was gone for five or six hours on Saturdays, and she complained that the time would be better spent with the kids, or doing errands. Roger believed that he deserved at least one chunk of time for himself after his tiring weeks, but he worried guiltily that Rachel had a legitimate point. After all, she took no comparable time for herself. The irony was that even with the golf, his weekends at home rarely left him feeling restored or renewed.

THE FIGHT TO FOCUS

The way that Roger managed his energy physically and emotionally helped to account for his third performance barrier: poor focus. Fatigue, unhappiness with his boss, frustration with Rachel, guilt about not spending more time with his children and the increased demands of his new job all made it difficult for him to stay focused mentally at work. Managing his time, which had never been much of an issue when he worked primarily as a salesman, was significantly more difficult now that he was expected to supervise forty people in four states. For the first time in his career, Roger found that he was distracted and inefficient.

On a typical day in the office, Roger received between fifty and seventy-five emails, and at least two dozen voice mails. Because he traveled as much as half of the time, he began carrying a BlackBerry. That made it possible to pick up his email anytime, anywhere. The problem was that he found himself forever responding to other people's issues and rarely setting his own agenda. Email also affected his attention span. He found it increasingly difficult to sustain concentration on any given task for long. Where he once thought of himself as creative and resourceful—he had designed the customer-tracking software that the whole office now used—there seemed to be no time anymore for longer-term projects. Instead, Roger lived his life from email to email, demand to demand, crisis to crisis. He rarely took breaks and his focus seemed to deteriorate as the day wore on.

Like nearly everyone he knew, Roger rarely left his work at the office. On his commute home at the end of the day, he usually spent his time on the cell phone returning calls. He answered email in the evenings and on the weekends. During the family's first European vacation the previous summer, Roger had felt compelled to check his voice mail and email every day. The prospect of returning home to a thousand unread emails and two hundred voice mails seemed worse, he told himself, than taking an hour out of each vacation day to stay current. The result was that Roger almost never disconnected completely from work.

WHAT REALLY MATTERS?

The truth was that Roger now spent so much of his life responding to external demands that he had lost touch with any sense of what he really wanted from life. When we asked what gave him the greatest sense of passion and meaning in his life, he came up empty. He didn't feel much passion at work, he admitted, even though his authority and his stature had increased. He didn't feel much at home, even though it was clear that he loved his wife and children and considered them his highest priorities. The powerful source of energy that can be derived from connecting to a clear sense of purpose simply wasn't available to Roger. Unmoored from deeply held values, he didn't have much motivation to take better care of himself physically, or to control his impatience, or even to prioritize his time and focus his attention. With so much to keep him busy, he spent very little energy reflecting on the choices that he had made. Thinking about his life only made him uncomfortable anyway, since nothing seemed likely to change.

Roger had nearly everything that he once thought he wanted from life, but more often than not what he felt was tired and frustrated, overworked and underappreciated. Above all, Roger told us, he felt like a victim of factors beyond his control.

I am a good guy, a decent guy, and I'm doing the best I can for my family. Sure I'm struggling, but I'm just trying to meet my responsibilities. I've got house payments and car payments and I'm trying to save for college for the kids. I would love to stay in shape, but between my commute and the hours I put in at work, I just can't find the time. It's true I've put on some weight, but when you live your life on the run, it's hard to eat healthy meals. Yeah, I eat snacks during the day, but how bad are a couple of cookies and an occasional bowl of frozen yogurt? A cigarette or two a day and a couple of drinks in the evening are just small pleasures that help take the edge off. It's not like I'm addicted.

I probably do get frustrated and lose my temper more often than I should at work, but that's not who I really am. I'm not getting much support, and the cutbacks at the company aren't making things any easier. It's hard to be focused and excited when you're under so much pressure.

I feel very guilty about not spending more time with my kids, and I definitely owe them more than I'm giving. Rachel is right that even when I'm there, I'm not really there. But then, neither is she. I miss having time with my wife and I do sometimes feel a little neglected, but then I realize she's got plenty on her plate too.

I definitely wish I felt better about my life, but I'm not sure what I should be doing differently. It could be a lot worse, I'll tell you that. Half of the people in my office are divorced. Last week a forty-two-year-old guy down the hall dropped dead of a heart attack—right at his desk. I just try to keep moving forward, put one foot in front of the other. This isn't exactly how I imagined things were going to be, but if there's a better way, I haven't figured it out.

CHAPTER 3

THE PULSE OF HIGH PERFORMANCE: BALANCING STRESS AND RECOVERY

The concept of maximizing performance by alternating periods of activity with periods of rest was first advanced by Flavius Philostratus (a.d. 170–245), who wrote training manuals for Greek athletes. Russian sports scientists resurrected the concept in the 1960s and began applying it with stunning success to their Olympic athletes. Today, "work-rest" ratios lie at the heart of periodization, a training method used by elite athletes throughout the world.

The science of periodization has become more precise and more sophisticated over the years, but the basic concept hasn't changed since it was first advanced nearly two thousand years ago. Following a period of activity, the body must replenish fundamental biochemical sources of energy. This is called "compensation" and when it occurs, energy expended is recovered. Increase the intensity of the training or the performance demand, and it is necessary to commensurately increase the amount of energy renewal. Fail to do so and the athlete will experience a measurable deterioration in performance.

Energy is simply the capacity to do work. Our most fundamental need as human beings is to spend and recover energy.

We need energy to perform, and recovery is more than the absence of work. It serves not just health and happiness, but also performance. Nearly every elite athlete we have worked with over the years has come to us with performance problems that could be traced to an imbalance between the expenditure and the recovery of energy. They were either overtraining or undertraining in one or more dimensions—physically, emotionally, mentally or spiritually. Both overtraining and undertraining have performance consequences that include persistent injuries and sickness, anxiety, negativity and anger, difficulty concentrating, and loss of passion. We achieved our breakthroughs with athletes by helping them to more skillfully manage energy—pushing themselves to systematically increase capacity in whatever dimension it was insufficient, but also to build in regular recovery as part of their training regimens.

Balancing stress and recovery is critical not just

in competitive sports, but also in managing energy in all facets of our lives. When we expend energy, we draw down our reservoir. When we recover energy, we fill it back up. Too much energy expenditure without sufficient recovery eventually leads to burnout and breakdown. (Over-use it and lose it.) Too much recovery without sufficient stress leads to atrophy and weakness. (Use it or lose it.) Just think about an arm placed in a cast for an extended period of time in order to protect it from the "stress" to which it is ordinarily subjected. In a very short time, the muscles of the arm begin to atrophy from disuse. The benefits of a sustained fitness program decrease significantly after just one week of inactivity—and disappear altogether in as few as four weeks.

The same process occurs emotionally, mentally and spiritually. Emotional depth and resilience depend on active engagement with others and with our own feelings. Mental acuity diminishes in the absence of ongoing intellectual challenge. Spiritual energy capacity depends on regularly revisiting our deepest values and holding ourselves accountable in our behavior. Full engagement requires cultivating a dynamic balance between the expenditure of energy (stress) and the renewal of energy (recovery) in all dimensions.

We call this rhythmic wave oscillation, and it represents the fundamental pulse of life.

44

The more powerful our pulse, the more fully engaged we can be. The same is true organizationally. To the degree that leaders and managers build cultures around continuous work—whether that means several-hour meetings, or long days, or the expectation that people will work in the evenings and on weekends—performance is necessarily compromised over time. Cultures that encourage people to seek intermittent renewal not only inspire greater commitment, but also more productivity.

Instead, most of us tend to live far more linear lives. We assume that we can spend energy indefinitely in some dimensions—often the mental and emotional—and that we can perform effectively without investing much energy at all in others—most commonly the physical and the spiritual. We become flat liners.

THE PULSE OF LIFE

Nature itself has a pulse, a rhythmic, wavelike movement between activity and rest. Think about the ebb and flow of the tides, the movement between seasons, and the daily rising and setting of the sun. Likewise, all organisms follow life-sustaining rhythms—birds migrating, bears hibernating, squirrels gathering nuts, and fish spawning, all of them at predictable intervals.

So, too, human beings are guided by rhythms—both those dictated by nature and those encoded in our genes. Seasonal affective disorder (SAD) is an illness that is attributable both to changes in seasonal rhythms and to the body's inability to adapt. Our breathing, brain waves, body temperature, heart rates, hormone levels and blood pressure all have healthy (and unhealthy) rhythmic patterns.

**We are oscillatory beings
in an oscillatory universe.
Rhythmicity is our inheritance.**

Oscillation occurs even at the most basic levels of our being. Healthy patterns of activity and rest lie at the heart of our capacity for full engagement, maximum performance and sustained health. Linearity, by contrast, ultimately leads to dysfunction and death. Just picture for a moment the undulating wave form of a healthy EEG or EKG—and then think about the implications of their opposite: a flat line.

At the broadest level, our activity and rest patterns are tied to circadian rhythms (*circa dies*, "around a day"), which cycle approximately every twenty-four hours. In the early 1950s, researchers Eugene Aserinsky and Nathan Kleitman discovered that sleep occurs in smaller cycles of 90- to 120-minute segments. We move from light sleep, when brain activity is intense and dreaming occurs, to deeper sleep, when the brain is more quiescent and the deepest restoration takes place.

This rhythm is called the "basic rest-activity cycle" (BRAC). In the 1970s, further research showed that a version of the same 90- to 120-minute cycles—ultradian rhythms (*ultra dies*, "many times a day")—operates in our waking lives.

These ultradian rhythms help to account for the ebb and flow of our energy throughout the day. Physiological measures such as heart rate, hormonal levels, muscle tension and brain-wave activity all increase during the first part of the cycle—and so does alertness. After an hour or so, these measures start to decline. Somewhere between 90 and 120 minutes, the body begins to crave a period of rest and recovery. Signals include a desire to yawn and stretch, hunger pangs, increased tension, difficulty concentrating, an inclination to procrastinate or fantasize, and a higher incidence of mistakes. We are capable of overriding these natural cycles, but only by summoning the fight-or-flight response and flooding our bodies with stress hormones that are designed to help us handle emergencies.

The long-term cost is that toxins build up inside us. We can only push so hard for so long without breaking down and burning out. Stress hormones that circulate chronically in our bodies may be temporarily energizing, but over time they prompt symptoms such as hyperactivity, aggressiveness, impatience, irritability, anger, self-absorption and insensitivity to others. Override the need for oscillation long enough and the symptoms may extend to headaches, back pain, gastrointestinal disorders, and ultimately to heart attacks and even death.

Because the body craves oscillation, we will often turn to artificial means to make waves when our lives become too linear. When we lack sufficient energy to meet the demands in our lives, for example, we turn to stimulants such as caffeine, cocaine and amphetamines. When we can't relax naturally, we may begin to rely on alcohol, marijuana and sleeping pills to cool down. If you are drinking several cups of coffee to stay alert during the day and a couple of drinks or several glasses of wine to disengage in the evening, you are simply masking your own linearity.

THE TIME BETWEEN POINTS

To live like a sprinter is to break life down into a series of manageable intervals consistent with our own physiological needs and with the periodic rhythms of nature. This insight first crystallized for Jim when he was working with world-class tennis players. As a performance psychologist, his goal was to understand the factors that set apart the greatest competitors in the world from the rest of the pack. Jim spent hundreds of hours watching top players and studying tapes of their matches. To his growing frustration, he could detect almost no significant differences in their competitive habits during points. It was only when he began

48

to notice what they did between points that he suddenly saw a difference. While most of them were not aware of it, the best players had each built almost exactly the same set of routines between points. These included the way they walked back to the baseline after a point; how they held their heads and shoulders; where they focused their eyes; the pattern of their breathing; and even the way they talked to themselves.

It dawned on Jim that these players were instinctively using the time between points to maximize their recovery. Many lower-ranked competitors, he began to see, had no recovery routines at all. When he hooked up the top players to EKG telemetry, which allowed him to monitor their heart rates, he made another startling discovery. In the sixteen to twenty seconds between points in a match, the heart rates of top competitors dropped as much as twenty beats per minute. By building highly efficient and focused recovery routines, these players had found a way to derive extraordinary energy renewal in a very short period of time. Because lesser competitors had no comparable routines between points, their heart rates often remained at high levels throughout their matches regardless of their level of fitness. The best competitors were using rituals to recover more efficiently and to better prepare for each upcoming point.

The performance consequences of instituting precise between-point rituals were dramatic.

Imagine two players of relatively equal talent and fitness in the third hour of a match. One has been regularly recovering between points, while the other has not. Clearly, the second player will be far more physically fatigued. In turn, fatigue has a cascade effect. A tired player is more susceptible to negative emotions such as anger and frustration, which will likely push his heart rate still higher, and likely lead to muscular tension. Physical fatigue also makes it far more difficult to concentrate. The same phenomenon applies even for those of us who work in sedentary jobs. Imagine that you have been sitting for long and continuous hours at your desk, operating under very high pressure. Fatigue is a likely consequence, and so is susceptibility to negative emotions and to distraction, all of which ultimately undermine performance.

In tennis, Jim's research proved this in measurable ways. The more linear or unvarying players' heart rates became, the worse they tended to play and the more likely it was that they lost their matches. Too much energy expenditure without sufficient recovery caused their heart rates to become chronically elevated. Their performance was equally compromised when their heart rates remained chronically low—typically a sign that they were not committed enough or had given up the fight.

Even in a sport such as golf, which requires very little expenditure of physical energy, rituals that balance energy expenditure with recovery are critical. Jack Nicklaus was remarkable for his skill and consistency, but also for his remarkable ability to analyze the elements that contributed to his success:

I was blessed with the ability to focus intensely on whatever I'm doing through most distraction and usually to the exclusion of whatever else might otherwise preoccupy me. Nevertheless, I can't concentrate on nothing but golf shots for the time it takes to play 18 holes. Even if I could, I suspect the drain of mental energy would make me pretty fuzzy-headed long before the last putt went down. In consequence, I've developed a regimen that allows me to move from peaks of concentration into valleys of relaxation and back again as necessary.

My focus begins to sharpen as I walk onto the tee, then steadily intensifies as I complete the process of analysis and evaluation that produces a clear-cut strategy for every shot I play. It then peaks as I set up to the ball and execute the swing when, ideally, my mind picture of what I'm trying to do is both totally exclusionary and totally positive.

Unless the tee shot finds serious trouble, when I might immediately start processing possible recoveries, I descend into a valley as I leave the tee, either through casual conversation with a fellow competitor or by letting my mind dwell on whatever happens into it. I try to adhere to this pattern whether I'm playing my best or worst, but obviously have to work harder at it when things aren't going well.

Balancing stress and recovery is valuable in any performance venue. In 1998, for example, the United States Army undertook a study to assess productivity during warfare. The measure was how many shells a gunnery crew could land on a target during a three-day period. One crew was told to shoot as many shells as it could manage over the entire three days. The second crew was told to take intermittent naps. For the first day, the nonstop shooters landed more shells on the target than their colleagues. By the second day, the accuracy of the nonstop shooters progressively waned and the intermittent nappers gained the lead for good.

Periods of recovery are likewise intrinsic to creativity and to intimate connection. Sounds become music in the spaces between notes, just as words are created by the spaces between letters. It is in the spaces between work that love, friendship, depth and dimension are nurtured. Without time for recovery, our lives become a blur of doing unbalanced by much opportunity for being.

RECOVERY AT WORK

Several years ago, the magazine *Fast Company* asked a series of successful professionals to talk about how they avoided burnout in the face of highly demanding jobs. Nearly every one described very specific routines that they had instituted to insure they regularly renewed themselves. Maggie Wilderotter, the president of Wink Communications, which develops interactive forms of television, developed something that she called a "lion hunt." "I prowl through the office, asking people what they're working on," she explained. "This gives me a chance to connect with employees whom I don't usually talk to. Lion hunts are incredibly relaxing because—even if they last just thirty minutes—they take me away from a schedule that requires me to push, push, push. I've never burned out because I don't let myself get to that point. You've got to be able to pace yourself and allow time for plenty of breaks. . . . Time is a finite resource and we all place infinite demands on it. I view time as an opportunity, as a chance to make choices about how I spend that resource."

Carisa Bianchi, president and CEO of the advertising company TBWA/Chiat/Day in San Francisco, builds recovery into her frequent travel. "I never work on airplanes—no computer, no phone, nothing," she said. "I read books and magazines and I listen to music—things that I don't usually have the time to do. You can always find reasons to work. There will always be one more thing to do, but when people don't take time out, they stop being productive." For Joe Gibbs, a former pro football coach who now runs a race-car company, recovery rituals focus around vacations. "On my calendar, I mark the days on which I tend to get away with my family," he explained. "They're marked with big yellow X's. We take a four-day weekend each month. Around Christmastime we spend nine days either skiing or vacationing someplace warm."

Bill Norman, executive vice president of the furniture company Herman Miller, described how he meticulously manages his schedule to maximize productivity on the job by minimizing distractions and building in plenty of time for energy renewal. "I stopped using voice mail six or seven years ago and I don't use a cell phone at all," he explained. "I know people for whom work is their life, their sole interest. But I think it's very important to do things outside of work that you enjoy. I enjoy photographing landscapes and taking close-up nature shots. It refreshes me and helps me stay focused. Photography exercises a set of creative muscles in my brain that don't necessarily get worked out in business—the ones that develop your intuitive mind, which can be critical for on-the-job decision making."

RENEWING ORGANIZATIONAL ENERGY

Balancing stress and recovery can be especially powerful on an organizational level. Bruce F. runs a division of a large telecommunications company and he came through our program with members of his top team. Along the way, it emerged that he liked to hold meetings that ran as long as three to four hours without a break. Immensely energetic himself, Bruce acknowledged that there was a macho element to these marathons, but he also told us that he considered the ability to sustain concentration over long periods a key measure of a strong executive. We pointed out that if his goal was to maximize productivity, he simply wasn't managing his team's energy efficiently. Given his demands, his executives might well force themselves to hang in at long meetings, and some would obviously do so more effectively than others. None of them, however, could possibly be as focused and sharp at the end of four nonstop hours as they had been at the start of the meeting.

At first Bruce was skeptical about the whole notion of recovery. He was moved, however, by the story of Jim's between-point research and most especially by the quality of recovery that players were able to get in a very short period of time. When Bruce left us, he decided to experiment with building brief periods of recovery into his own workdays. Almost immediately, he discovered that he not only returned from his breaks more physically energized, but also that he felt more positive emotionally. An enthusiastic man by nature, Bruce became a true believer in the power of intermittent recovery. He continued to experiment with different forms, and eventually settled on two that took his mind completely off work and proved to be especially restorative.

Bruce's first recovery strategy was walking up and down a dozen flights of stairs in his office building. The second was juggling. Shortly after leaving us, he began teaching himself to juggle using three balls. Within six months, he could handle a half-dozen, and the experience took his mind completely off work and gave him a pure sense of joy. Several weeks after his visit to us, Bruce completely changed the way that he conducted meetings. He began scheduling an inviolable fifteen-minute break every ninety minutes—and he requested that no one discuss business during the breaks. "People took a cue from me," Bruce said. "Our recovery breaks just loosened up our whole organization. We get more done at our meetings now in less time, and we have more fun doing it."

A WORLD HOSTILE TO REST

Without being aware of it, Roger B. was living a highly linear life. By working long hours and rarely shutting down, even when he was home, he was relentlessly spending mental energy without getting much recovery. Fatigue prompted anxiety, irritability and self-doubt, and he had very few positive sources of emotional renewal, even from his primary relationships. In the language of sports, Roger was overtraining mentally and emotionally and undertraining physically and spiritually. Because he expended precious little energy in activity and exercise, he had progressively lost endurance, strength and resilience. Because he had grown disconnected from deeply held values or a sense of purpose, the spiritual dimension represented another flat line in his life—a potential source of energy that he simply had not cultivated.

Roger was not much different than many of us, in part because the choices he was making are so socially sanctioned. We live in a world that celebrates work and activity, ignores renewal and recovery, and fails to recognize that both are necessary for sustained high performance. As physiologist Martin Moore-Ede, the president of Circadian Technologies and the author of *The Twenty-Four-Hour Society*, puts it:

At the heart of the problem is a fundamental conflict between the demands of our man-made civilization and the very design of the human brain and body. . . . Our bodies were designed to hunt by day, sleep at night and never travel more than a few dozen miles from sunrise to sunset. Now we work and play at all hours, whisk off by jet to the far side of the globe, make life-or-death decisions or place orders on foreign stock exchanges in the wee hours of the morning. The pace of technological innovation is outstripping the ability of the human race to understand the consequences. We are machine-centered in our thinking—focused on the optimization of technology and equipment—rather than human-centered—focused on the optimization of human alertness and performance.

At the most practical level, our capacity to be fully engaged depends on our ability to periodically disengage. For most of us, this requires an entirely new way of thinking about how to manage our energy. Many of us treat life as a marathon that doesn't end until it finally ends for good. Along the way, we learn strategies for conserving our limited resources. This may mean expending energy at a certain steady level at work but rarely fully engaging, or pushing very intensely on the job and then having little energy left to invest at home. Or it may mean slowly disengaging in every sphere of life, as Roger had begun to do.

The inexorable advances in technology—meant to help us stay more connected—often serve instead to keep us from ever fully disconnecting. Consider the way that Robert Iger, the president of the Walt Disney Company, has described the

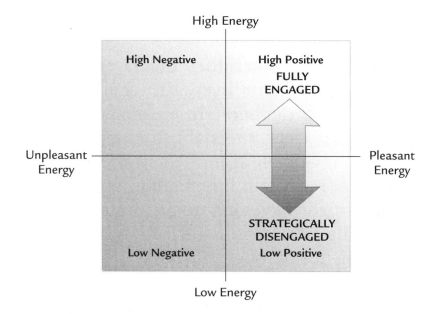

impact of email on his life: "It's just completely changed the rhythm of my workday. I try to avoid turning on the computer when I wake up, because I know if I do, I won't read my newspapers. By the time I do log on, around 6 a.m., twenty-five messages have accumulated since I last checked before going to sleep. It really affects your attention span. All of a sudden, you find yourself turning around in your chair just to see what's there. Without thinking about it, you start answering them, and before long, forty minutes have gone by. I now find myself purposely avoiding meetings just to handle the increasing volume of email. The umbilical cord to work is longer than it's ever been." Iger is scarcely alone. A study conducted by America Online in 2000 found that 47 percent of its subscribers took their laptops on vacation, and 26 percent continued to check their email every day.

Because we have overridden the natural rhythms that once defined our lives, the challenge is to consciously and deliberately create new boundaries. We must learn to establish stopping points in our days, inviolable times when we step off the track, cease processing information and shift our attention from achievement to restoration. Moore-Ede calls this a "time cocoon." As Wayne Muller puts it in his lovely book *Sabbath*:

> The busier we are, the more important we seem to ourselves and, we imagine, to others. To be unavailable to our friends and family, to be unable to find time for the sunset (or even to know the sun has set at all), to whiz through our obligations without time for a mindful breath, this has become the model of a successful life.

We have lost connection, Muller argues, to the simple but profound message of the Twenty-third Psalm: "He makes me lie down in green pastures; He leads me beside still waters. He restores my soul." Intermittently disengaging is what allows us to passionately reengage.

STRESS ADDICTION

Working at a feverish pace without breaks may actually be addictive. Stress hormones such as adrenaline, noradrenaline and cortisol fuel arousal and create a seductive rush—the so-called adrenaline high. When we operate at a high enough intensity for long enough, we progressively lose the capacity to shift to any other gear. Our natural inclination is to push harder when demand increases. Over time we resist precisely what would make us more effective: taking breaks and seeking restoration. In effect, we get stuck in overdrive, unable to turn off the engine.

Take Dick Wolf, the executive producer of *Law & Order* and half a dozen other network television series. He once told a reporter that he had worked as many as thirty-four days consecutively, and gone as long as four years without a vacation. "The scary thing," he explained, "is that I've lost the ability to shut off, even on a weekend, even when I'm up in Maine, where we have a vacation house away from it all, and even if I have nothing to do when I'm there. I find myself feeling guilty if I'm not working. I'll think, 'I really should be doing something.' And I'll almost always find something to do. It's an inability to pull the plug and just vegetate." It never dawned on Wolf that what he called vegetating might actually be a powerful way to refill his energy reservoir.

For Mark Ethridge, a former managing editor of

The Charlotte Observer, the costs of his own addiction seemed clearer. "More and more what I find is that you don't really live in the present anymore," he explained. "You're never fully engaged in what you're doing at any given moment, because what you really want to do is finish it in order to get on to something else. You kind of skim along the surface of life. It's very frustrating."

Any addictive behavior—including work—prompts a highly linear form of energy expenditure. It is no wonder that efforts to rehabilitate drug and alcohol addicts are referred to as "recovery." "Overwork is this decade's cocaine, the problem without a name," says Bryan Robinson, who has written widely about the phenomenon and estimates that as many as 25 percent of Americans have the addiction. "Workaholism is an obsessive-compulsive disorder," he writes, "that manifests itself through self-imposed demands, an inability to regulate work habits and an overindulgence in work—to the exclusion of most other life activities." Unlike most addictions, workaholism is often admired, encouraged and materially well rewarded. The costs are more long term. Researchers have found that those who describe themselves as workaholics have a significantly higher than average incidence of alcohol abuse, divorce and stress-related illnesses.

Under the pretext of research for this book, Tony decided to attend a Workaholics Anonymous meeting in New York City, near his home. In truth, he was also curious to see if his own work habits fit the definition. When Tony got to the meeting, there were four other people gathered around a table in a church basement. It turned out that the group's size hadn't increased significantly since its founding a decade ago—hardly a surprise when you think about it. How many workaholics would be willing to take time out to attend a meeting about working too hard? This one lasted an hour, and as Tony was leaving, one of the participants approached him. "Welcome to the French Resistance," the man said with a sly smile. "There are five million workaholics in New York, and you've just met the only four who are in recovery."

DEATH FROM OVERWORK

It is not the intensity of energy expenditure that produces burnout, impaired performance and physical breakdown, but rather the duration of expenditure without recovery. In Japan, the term karoshi can be translated literally as "death from overwork"—most commonly from heart attack and stroke. The first case of karoshi was reported in 1969. The Japanese Ministry of Labor began to publish statistics on the syndrome in 1987 and the National Defense Council for Victims of Karoshi was launched the following year. Some ten thousand deaths a year in Japan are now attributed to karoshi, and research shows that there are five key factors:

- Extremely long hours that interfere with normal recovery and rest patterns
- Night work that interferes with normal recovery and rest patterns
- Working without holidays or breaks
- High-pressure work without breaks
- Extremely demanding physical labor and continuously stressful work

What these five factors have in common is a pattern of chronic energy expenditure and an absence of intermittent recovery. The number of Japanese workers who put in more than 3,120 hours a year—an average of more than sixty hours a week—increased from three million, or 15 percent of the workforce, in 1975, to seven million, or 24 percent, in 1988. One case study described a worker who died suddenly at the age of forty-five. It turned out that he had worked thirteen consecutive days, including six successive night shifts. His job was assembling engine parts for Mazda Motor Company, and he worked on a line where the speed was two minutes per car. The methods devised to assure maximum efficiency were so unforgiving that workers had almost no time at all to recover. "Under this production method," the researchers concluded, "the worker resembles a mouse running helplessly in a rotating wheel in order to avoid electric shock. . . ." No comparable research on the health or consequences of overwork exists in the United States, but America is the only country in the world in which employees work more hours per week than the Japanese.

Nancy Woodhull was the epitome of high energy, a founding publisher of *USA Today* and a highly successful executive with a very busy and varied life. "I'm not the type of person," she once explained, "who can just sit around the pool and not do anything, so I take a Dictaphone to the pool, and when I have ideas, I can record them. Not being able to do that would be very stressful to me. People will say to me, 'Nancy, relax, recharge your energy,' and I say, 'I'm being energized by getting these ideas down.' Having access to a Dictaphone allows you to be more productive. So does having a cellular phone, and so does having a computer. You take all these tools and there really is no need for downtime. Anyone can find me, anywhere, anytime."

Less than ten years after she described this modus operandi, Woodhull died of cancer. She was fifty-two years old. There is no way of determining conclusively whether there was any relationship between Woodhull's work habits and her early death, but her profile was not significantly different from many of the Japanese who die from karoshi. There is also considerable evidence that highly linear forms of behavior—too much eating, too little sleep, too much hostility, too little physical activity, too much continuous stress—lead to a higher incidence of illness and even early death.

Basedow's disease represents a precursor to karoshi—a response to highly linear stress. It shows up especially in athletes who have over-trained, pushing themselves relentlessly with very limited recovery. Among its symptoms are increased resting heart rate, decreased appetite, disturbed sleep, higher resting blood pressure, irritability, emotional instability, loss of motivation and increased incidence of injuries and infections. We see many of these symptoms in the executives with whom we work.

William D., a midlevel manager at a large consumer company, came to us with one of the most common performance barriers that we see. In the mornings, he was full of energy, and he charged through his obligations at high intensity. He estimated that he got more than 70 percent of his day's work done before lunch. By early afternoon, however, his energy flagged considerably, and with it his enthusiasm and his focus. By the time he got home, he felt completely wiped out and complained that he had nothing left to give. He wondered if he might have Lyme disease or chronic fatigue syndrome and went to his doctor to be checked out. The tests came back negative. What then was the explanation? Put simply, demand was increasing while his capacity was diminishing. At fifty, William wasn't as resilient as he had been at forty or thirty. To maintain his current capacity, he had to be more attentive to intermittent recovery.

In the aftermath of his work with us, William made one relatively simple change in the way he worked. He began taking a break every 90 to 120 minutes, during which he ate something, drank some water and took at least a brief walk. Based on this change alone, within two weeks William estimated a 30 percent increase in his energy in the afternoons.

WHEN WHAT YOU HAVE IS NOT ENOUGH

Regularly renewing our energy insures that we can sustain full engagement—so long as demand remains constant. But what happens when increased demand overwhelms our capacity and even a full tank is not enough?

The answer is paradoxical—and precisely the opposite of what you've probably been told most of your life. To build capacity, we must systematically expose ourselves to more stress—followed by adequate recovery. Challenging a muscle past its current limits prompts a phenomenon known as supercompensation. Faced with a demand that exceeds the muscle's current capacity, the body responds by building more muscle fibers in anticipation of the next stimulus.

**We grow at all levels
by expending energy beyond
our normal limits,
and then recovering.**

The same is true, we have found, of "muscles" at all levels—emotional, mental and spiritual. The catch is that we instinctively resist pushing beyond our current comfort zones. Homeostasis is a state of equilibrium—the biological maintenance of the status quo. When we challenge our equilibrium, discomfort serves as an early warning system, alerting us that we are entering uncharted territory and urging us to return to safe ground. In the case of real danger, the experience of alarm is useful and self-protective. Subject a muscle to excessive demand, for example, and you risk significant injury. But expose the muscle to ordinary demand and it won't grow.

**Expanding capacity requires
a willingness to endure
short-term discomfort in the service
of long-term reward.**

The same paradoxical phenomenon applies to achieving long-term satisfaction and well-being. "We can experience pleasure without any investment of psychic energy, whereas enjoyment happens only as a result of unusual investments of attention . . . ," writes psychologist Mihaly

Csikszentmihalyi, author of *Flow*. "The best moments [in our lives] usually occur when a person's body or mind is stretched to its limits in a voluntary effort to accomplish something difficult and worthwhile." Most of us have experienced this phenomenon. The intensity of pleasure that we derive from a given activity tends to diminish over time. Much as we fear change, the deepest satisfaction comes from our willingness to expose ourselves to new challenges and engage in novel experiences.

The willingness to challenge our comfort zones depends partly on our degree of underlying security. To whatever degree we are consumed by anxious concerns and attempts to fill deficits—for energy, or material security, or self-esteem—we are less willing to expose ourselves to any discomfort. When there isn't much fuel in our tanks and our inner experience is that we feel threatened, we tend to hoard the energy we have and use our limited stores in the service of self-protection. We refer to this phenomenon as defense spending. Accurately assessing the level of threat in our lives is critical if we are to continue to grow rather than forever defending what we have.

VOLUNTARY AND INVOLUNTARY STORMS

Throughout our lives, we face storms of varying levels of intensity in all dimensions: physical, emotional, mental and spiritual. When the force of the storm is greater than we can handle physically, the result might be a broken bone, or a heart attack. The first imperative is to protect the injured limb or organ from further stress. A physician puts a broken arm in a cast to protect the bone as it heals, or prescribes bed rest immediately following a heart attack. But we can't leave the cast on or remain sedentary for too long. Inactivity very quickly causes atrophy and loss of strength.

Rehabilitation is the process by which we systematically build back capacity. The approach is always the same: gradual and incremental exposure to increasing doses of stress. Push too hard or too quickly, and you are likely to get hurt again. This is true of a broken arm or a damaged heart, but it applies equally to other dimensions in which sudden storms have sapped our strength. If you are the victim of a violent crime, or lose a loved one, or get fired from a job, the first need is for healing, recovery and time to regroup. Rebuilding energy capacity requires gradually reexposing ourselves to the demands of the world that dealt us the setback in the first place. So long as sufficient healing has occurred, it is often possible to build capacity past our previous limits.

The same principle applies to building capacity by conscious choice. Think about an infant venturing away from his mother, but turning back frequently to make sure that she is still there. The infant is testing his current comfort zone. His mother's smile of reassurance is a source of emotional recovery and positive renewal. It makes him feel empowered to take a few steps further into the unknown, to continue expanding his capacity. Without that reassurance, he comes scurrying back to his mother. We are not so different as adults. When we feel threatened, we tend to retreat. Recovery is a means of detoxifying and refueling so that we can return to the storm with renewed energy. When we feel challenged rather than threatened, we are more willing to extend ourselves, even if that means taking some risk and experiencing some discomfort along the way.

When we first suggested to Roger B. that he lacked sufficient capacity in part because he hadn't exposed himself to sufficient stress, he was incredulous. "My life is more stressful than ever," he insisted. "I'm getting less help from my boss, and I've got more people to supervise, fewer resources and more competition. If what you're saying is right, how come I'm not getting stronger?" Many of our clients initially raise the same question.

The answer, we tell them, is that the key to expanding capacity is both to push beyond one's ordinary limits and to regularly seek recovery, which is when growth actually occurs. There was no area of Roger's life in which he was doing both. At the physical and spiritual level, he wasn't spending enough energy to build capacity. Because he was undertraining those muscles, they continued to atrophy.

In the other two dimensions—mental and emotional—Roger was overtraining, subjecting himself to excessive stress without sufficient intermittent recovery. The result was that he felt overwhelmed. His solution was simply to keep pushing. What he needed was time to detoxify and change channels in order to periodically renew mentally and emotionally. Roger was pushing himself too hard in some dimensions and not hard enough in others. The ultimate consequence was the same: diminished capacity in the face of rising demand.

BEAR IN MIND

- Our most fundamental need as human beings is to spend and recover energy. We call this oscillation.
- The opposite of oscillation is linearity: too much energy expenditure without recovery or too much recovery without sufficient energy expenditure.
- Balancing stress and recovery is critical to high performance both individually and organizationally.
- We must sustain healthy oscillatory rhythms at all four levels of what we term the "performance pyramid": physical, emotional, mental and spiritual.
- We build emotional, mental and spiritual capacity in precisely the same way that we build physical capacity. We must systematically expose

72

ourselves to stress beyond our normal limits, followed by adequate recovery.

• Expanding capacity requires a willingness to endure short-term discomfort in the service of long-term reward.

CHAPTER 4

PHYSICAL ENERGY: FUELING THE FIRE

The importance of physical energy seems obvious for athletes, construction workers and farmers. Because the rest of us are evaluated more by what we do with our minds than with our bodies, we tend to discount the role that physical energy plays in performance. In most jobs, the physical body has been completely cut off from the performance equation. In reality, physical energy is the fundamental source of fuel, even if our work is almost completely sedentary. It not only lies at the heart of alertness and vitality but also affects our ability to manage our emotions, sustain concentration, think creatively, and even maintain our commitment to whatever mission we are on. Leaders and managers make a fundamental mistake when they assume that they can overlook the physical dimension of energy and still expect those who work for them to perform at their best.

74

At the time we met Roger B., he had never thought much about managing his energy in any part of his life, and he gave virtually no attention to the physical dimension. He realized that he would probably feel better if he got more sleep and exercised regularly, but the way he saw it, he simply didn't have the time. He knew that his diet wasn't very healthy, but he couldn't summon much motivation to change. Instead, he tried not to think about the consequences of his choices. Mostly what Roger felt was busy—and numb.

At the most basic level, physical energy is derived from the interaction between oxygen and glucose. In practical terms, the size of our energy reservoir depends on the patterns of our breathing, the foods that we eat and when we eat them, the quantity and quality of our sleep, the degree to which we get intermittent recovery during the day, and the level of our fitness. Building a rhythmic balance between physical energy expenditure and recovery insures that the level of our energy reserves remains relatively constant. Pushing past our comfort zone—and then recovering—is a means by which to expand physical capacity wherever it is insufficient to meet demand.

The most important rhythms in our lives are the ones we typically take for granted—most notably breathing and eating. Few of us even think about breathing. Oxygen becomes precious only in those rare instances when we can't get enough—choking on a piece of food, getting caught in an ocean undertow, or suffering from a disease such as emphysema. Even significant changes in our pattern of breathing tend to go unnoticed. Anxiety and anger, for example, typically prompt faster and shallower breathing, which can be valuable in responding to an immediate threat. Very quickly, however, such a breathing pattern reduces our available energy and compromises our ability to restore mental and emotional equilibrium. The result can be a cycle that reinforces itself, which explains why one of the simplest antidotes to anger and anxiety is to take deep abdominal breaths.

The breath is a powerful tool for self-regulation—a means both to summon energy and to relax deeply. Extending the exhalation, for example, prompts a powerful wave of recovery. Breathing in to a count of three and out to a count of six, lowers arousal and quiets not just the body but also the mind and the emotions. Deep, smooth and rhythmic breathing is simultaneously a source of energy, alertness and focus as well as of relaxation, stillness and quiet—the ultimate healthy pulse.

STRATEGIC EATING

The second critical source of physical energy in our lives comes from the foods we eat. The costs of not eating enough—renewing energy with food that gets converted into glycogen—are clear. Most of us have not had much experience with prolonged hunger, but we all know the visceral feeling of being hungry and its impact on our ability to function effectively at all levels. On an empty stomach, it is difficult to be concerned with much besides food. Chronic overeating, on the other hand, represents too much "recovery," leads to obesity and compromised energy, and has both performance and health consequences. Foods high in fats, sugar and simple carbohydrates provide recovery, but in a much less efficient and energy-rich form than low-fat proteins and complex carbohydrates such as vegetables and grains.

Eating better obviously has benefits in and of itself, including losing weight, looking better and improving health, all of which may have positive energy consequences. Our primary aim is to help clients sustain a steady, high-octane source of energy throughout the day. When you awake in the mornings, after eight to twelve hours without eating, your blood glucose levels are at a low ebb, even if you don't feel consciously hungry. Eating breakfast is critically important. It not only increases blood glucose levels, but also jump-starts metabolism.

It is equally important to eat foods that are low on the glycemic index, which measures the speed with which sugar from specific foods is released into the bloodstream. (See Glycemic Index Examples in Resources.) A slower release provides a steadier source of energy. The low-glycemic breakfast foods that provide the highest octane and longest lasting source of energy, for example, include whole grains, proteins and low-glycemic fruits such as strawberries, pears, grapefruit and apples. By contrast, high-glycemic foods such as muffins or sugary cereals spike energy for short periods but prompt a crash in as few as thirty minutes. Even a breakfast traditionally viewed as healthy—an unbuttered bagel and a glass of orange juice—is very high on the glycemic index and therefore a poor source of sustaining energy.

The frequency with which we eat also influences our capacity to stay fully engaged and to sustain high performance. Eating five to six low calorie, highly nutritious "meals" a day insures a steady resupply of energy. Even the most energy rich foods won't fuel high performance for the four to eight hours that many of us frequently permit to pass between meals. In one study at New York's Mount Sinai Hospital, subjects were placed in an environment with no clocks or time cues. Provided with food, they were told to eat whenever they were hungry. They did so an average of once every ninety-six minutes.

Sustained performance depends not just on eating at regular intervals but also on eating only as much as you need to drive your energy for the next two to three hours. Portion control is critical both in managing weight and in regulating energy. It is just as problematic to eat too much, too often, as it is to eat too little, too infrequently. Snacks between meals should typically be between 100 and 150 calories and once again should focus on low-glycemic

HUNGER SCALE

10 Feel sick; hate thought of food

9 Too full to move

8 Feel sluggish; change into sweats

7 Feel drowsy; unbutton pants; loosen belt

6 Full; feel food in stomach

5 Satisfied; can't feel food in stomach; lasts 2–3 hours—the Ideal Performance State

4 Not hungry, but not satisfied; hunger within 2 hours

3 Hungry; stomach growling

2 Grumpy, losing concentration, light-headed

1 Mean, headaches, dizziness

0 So hungry you aren't hungry anymore

foods such as nuts and sunflower seeds, fruits, or half of a typical-size 200 calorie energy bar.

To maximize physical energy capacity, we must become more attuned to what satisfaction actually feels like—neither hungry nor stuffed. Most of us spend far too much time at one end of the scale or the other, often swinging wildly between the two extremes. (See Hunger Scale.) We allow too much time to elapse between meals and then compensate by eating too much at once. Because our energy requirements tend to diminish as evening approaches and our metabolism slows, it makes sense to eat more calories earlier in the day and fewer in the evening. In one study of children ages seven to twelve, for example, subjects were classified into five weight categories, from thin to obese. On average, they all consumed about the same number of calories per day. The one variable, it turned out, was that the children in the two heaviest categories ate less at breakfast and more at dinner than their leaner counterparts. In a second study at the University of Minnesota, researchers compared groups of people on a 2,000-calorie-a-day diet. Those who ate the largest percentage of their food earlier in the day felt less tired and lost 2.3 pounds a week more than those who ate the most later in the day.

Drinking water, we have found, is perhaps the most undervalued source of physical energy renewal. Unlike hunger, thirst is an inadequate barometer of need. By the time we feel thirsty, we may be long since dehydrated. A growing body of research suggests that drinking at least sixty-four ounces of water at intervals throughout the day serves performance in a range of important ways. Dehydrate a muscle by as little as 3 percent, for example, and it will lose 10 percent of its strength and 8 percent of its speed. Inadequate hydration also compromises concentration and coordination.

Drinking more water may even have health and longevity benefits. In a study of 20,000 people, Australian researchers found that those who drank five eight-ounce glasses of water a day were significantly less likely to die of coronary heart disease as those who drank two glasses of water or less. One possible reason is that dehydration may elevate risk factors such as blood viscosity. By contrast, the consumption of coffee and caffeinated sodas provided no statistically significant heart benefits. Like high-sugar foods, caffeinated drinks such as coffee, tea and diet colas provide temporary spikes of energy. Because caffeine is a diuretic, however, it prompts dehydration and fatigue in the long run.

GEORGE D.: LOW ENERGY

George D., forty-one, is a music company executive who had long taken enormous satisfaction from work that he found creatively challenging and exciting. Increasingly, however, he complained that he had lost his passion for work and that he lacked the boundless energy that fueled him through his twenties. His first obstacle was all too visible. At five feet, eleven inches, he weighed 240 pounds, at least 50 more than his ideal weight and nearly all of it added during the past decade. His body fat percentage was 30—more than 10 percent above the maximum acceptable level for a man his age. Imagine for a moment the energy consequences of dragging around an extra fifty pounds each day. On average, we find that our clients gain approximately ten pounds a decade following college. Thirty-five percent of Americans are currently overweight, and another 25 percent are obese, according to the U.S. Department of Health and Human Services—an epidemic rise during the past twenty years. In George's case, we focused on how his eating habits might be affecting his basic energy levels and his sense of passion.

It turned out that George's routine during the past several years was to eat lightly for much of the day, surviving mostly on coffee in the mornings and a salad or a bagel for lunch. Around 3:00 p.m. he would begin to feel both deeply fatigued and famished. When sweets weren't available on his floor, he ran up to the employee cafeteria, long after it had stopped serving full meals for lunch, and grabbed a bag of chips and a piece of cake or a candy bar, rationalizing that he hadn't eaten breakfast or lunch. At night, he ate whatever his wife served. Because she knew he was hungry by the time he got home, she made enough for several helpings.

George's problems began with skipping breakfast, perhaps the most important meal of the day. As we noted earlier, a high-octane breakfast not only increases blood glucose levels but also jump-starts metabolism. George experimented with several breakfast foods before deciding to alternate

GEORGE D.

Performance Barrier: Low energy
Desired Outcome: Sustained high energy

RITUAL

7:00 A.M.: Breakfast: whole grain cereal or smoothie with protein powder

10:00 A.M.: Snack: Half of a low-sugar energy bar; or a handful of nuts; or a piece of fruit.

12:30 P.M.: Lunch: Salad bar at local gourmet deli

3:30 P.M.: Snack: Same as 10 A.M. above

7:00 P.M.: Dinner

8:30 P.M.: A sweets indulgence (e.g., frozen yogurt)

ONE-TIME ACTION STEPS

- Add energy bars, fruit, sunflower seeds, whole grain cereals, plain yogurt, protein powder and bottled water to regular shopping list
- Remove cookies, chips, crackers and other junk food from kitchen shelves
- Pack snacks for the week into briefcase on Sunday evening

each day between whole-grain cereal with plain yogurt and a smoothie: protein powder, skim milk, a banana, and strawberries or blueberries. He also limited himself to a single cup of coffee, and replaced the coffee mug that he was used to carrying around with a bottle of water. At mid-morning, he ate half of an energy bar or a handful of pumpkin seeds or mixed nuts, an ample supply of which he kept in a desk drawer and also in his briefcase. The latter was especially useful when he found himself stuck in an airport, or taking a long drive in his car.

For lunch, George found a gourmet food shop two blocks from his office that had a salad bar stocked with an appetizing array of fresh vegetables, fruits and other healthy items. Each day he was able to create a different salad that was healthy but also appealing and even included very small amounts of high fat foods that he liked, such as cheese. At 3:00 p.m. when he ordinarily would have gone to the cafeteria for chips and sweets, George reached into his desk for one of the energy-rich snacks that he hadn't eaten in the morning.

For as long as he could remember, the two experiences that George most associated with food were intense hunger and bloatedness. As he began to eat smaller amounts at regular two- to-three-hour intervals, it dawned on him that for the first time he felt satisfied. Carrying a water bottle wherever he went and sipping at it all day long helped to keep his hunger at bay.

George made no attempt to change the foods that he was eating for dinner, but he did ask his wife to make smaller portions. During the first thirty days that he was instituting his ritual, he consciously placed on his plate the exact amount of food that he intended to eat and no more. We subscribe to an 80–20 rule. If 80 percent of what you eat fuels performance and health, you can eat whatever you like for the other 20 percent—so long as you control the size of the portions.

Several times a week around 8:30, George indulged his sweet tooth with a half dozen Hershey kisses or a small cup of frozen yogurt. By his best estimate, George only moderately reduced his caloric intake with his new eating habits, but he completely shifted what he ate and when. By the end of a week on his new eating regimen, he felt a noticeable increase in his energy levels throughout the day. To his delight, having more energy improved his mood and his capacity for focus. As a bonus, George lost twenty-four pounds over the next six months and rarely felt deprived along the way. His body fat dropped to 23 percent. Without the extra weight, his energy levels continued to improve, and so did his sense of control over his life. He had occasional lapses, particularly at parties and over holidays, but at the end of a year, he had still kept most of the weight off and his capacity for work had increased markedly.

CIRCADIANS AND SLEEP

Other than eating and breathing, sleeping is the most important source of recovery in our lives. It is also the most powerful of the circadian rhythms that include body temperature, hormone levels and heart rates. The vast majority of our clients report that they are significantly sleep deprived. Few of them recognize just how dramatically insufficient sleep affects their performance and their level of engagement both at work and at home.

Even small amounts of sleep debt—insufficient recovery in our terms—have a significant impact on strength, cardiovascular capacity, mood and overall energy levels. Some fifty studies have shown that mental performance—reaction time, concentration, memory and logical/analytical reasoning—all decline steadily as sleep debt increases. Sleep needs vary by age, gender and genetic predisposition, but the broad scientific consensus is that the average human being needs seven to eight hours a night to function optimally. Several studies have shown that when human beings are placed in isolation, with no exposure to natural light or to clocks, they still sleep approximately seven to eight hours out of every twenty-four.

In one especially dramatic study, psychologist Dan Kripke and his colleagues studied the sleep patterns of one million people over six years. Mortality rates from nearly all causes of death were lowest among people who slept between seven and eight hours a night. For those sleeping less than four hours, mortality rates were two and a half times higher. For those sleeping more than ten hours the rates were one and a half times higher. In short, both too little recovery and too much recovery appear to significantly increase the risk of mortality.

The specific times that we sleep also affect our energy levels, health and performance. Numerous studies have shown that shift workers—meaning those who work at night—have twice the number of highway accidents as day workers and considerably more on-the-job accidents as well. Shift workers also suffer a far higher incidence of coronary artery disease and heart attacks than do day workers. On a broader scale, every one of the great industrial disasters of the past twenty years—Chernobyl, the Exxon Valdez, Bhopal, Three Mile Island—occurred in the middle of the night. For the most part, those in charge had worked very long hours and built up considerable sleep debt. The disastrous crash of the Challenger space shuttle in 1986, in which seven astronauts lost their lives, occurred after NASA officials made an ill-fated judgment to go ahead with the launch, having already worked for more than twenty consecutive hours.

**The longer, more continuously,
and later at night you work,
the less efficient and more
mistake-prone you become.**

In addition to its energy renewing function, sleep

is also a period during which substantial growth and repair occurs—most of it at the deepest level of sleep, when slow-wave delta brainwaves are dominant. During those periods, cell division is most active, the greatest number of growth hormones and repair enzymes are released and muscles that have been stressed during the day have an opportunity to regenerate. In short, we heal and grow most during the deepest periods of recovery.

There may be no more extreme example of deliberately overriding the human need for intermittent recovery than the long-standing system of training medical students to become physicians. They work in shifts as long as 36 consecutive hours and for as many as 120 hours in a week. In 1984, the journalist Sidney Zion brought a widely publicized lawsuit after his daughter Libby died following a visit to the emergency room of a New York City hospital. A grand jury ultimately concluded that she had received "woefully inadequate" care from inexperienced interns and residents operating on little or no sleep.

Three years after Libby Zion's death, the State of New York instituted new regulations that included limiting scheduled workweeks for residents (and other critical-care specialists) to no more than eighty hours and scheduled shifts to no more than twenty-four hours. In 2002, the national association that accredits physicians put the same twenty-four hour limit on maximum shifts for all of the nation's 100,000 medical residents. It was hardly a complete solution. In Japan, for example, the cause of death can be attributed to karoshi, or overwork, if a worker has put in twenty-four consecutive hours just before death. According to the National Academy of Sciences, medical errors, many of them at least partly caused by fatigue among doctors, account for nearly 100,000 deaths a year, more than from motor vehicle accidents, breast cancer and AIDS combined.

For years, medical school and hospital administrators have argued that compelling residents to work long hours makes them better able to handle the pressures that they will have to face as doctors. But try asking a hospital administrator whether he is comfortable driving on a highway at night alongside truck drivers who haven't slept for twenty-four hours; or flying on a plane in which a young pilot in training hasn't slept for thirty hours; or living in the vicinity of a nuclear plant in which new operators work in isolation for twelve-hour shifts through the night. The real reason that young physicians-in-training work such long shifts is economic. The cost of implementing the new post–Libby Zion regulations in New York state alone—mostly related to replacing lost hours of labor by residents—has been estimated to be in excess of $225 million a year.

A better understanding of how to efficiently manage stress-recovery ratios would likely eliminate much of that cost—and save many lives. Sleep researcher and physiologist Claudio Stampi undertook a study in which subjects were deprived of normal sleep, and instead took twenty- to-thirty-minute naps every four hours. Naps represent a form of strategic recovery. Stampi found that napping workers were able to maintain a surprisingly high level of alertness and productivity over twenty-four hours, even in the absence of a more prolonged sleep. The only caveat was that the naps had to be timed to insure that the subjects didn't fall into deeper stages of sleep. After more than thirty to forty minutes of sleep, many of them emerged feeling groggy and even more fatigued than if they hadn't napped at all.

JODY R.: POOR CONCENTRATION

A night owl, Jody R. struggled with getting to bed at a reasonable time each night and struggled even more with waking up in the morning. Her father had the same pattern, and Jody felt convinced that her sleep habits were encoded in her genes. She rarely got to sleep before 1:00 a.m. and she had to be up for work by 6:00 a.m. An ordinary night's sleep was five hours. The result was that she lived in a permanent state of fatigue and felt certain that it affected both her level of engagement and her ability to concentrate, especially in the mornings, when she typically felt groggy and out of it.

We asked Jody how she spent the last couple of hours each night, and she told us that she alternated between answering email, playing solitaire

JODY R.

Performance Barrier: Poor concentration, fatigue

Desired Outcome: High focus

RITUAL

10:00 P.M.: Bath
10:30 P.M.: Cup of chamomile tea
10:45 P.M.: Journal writing
11:00 P.M.: Reading
11:15 P.M.: Turn out lights
 6:00 A.M.: Wake up (alarm away from bed)
 6:15 A.M.: Fifteen-minute brisk walk
 6:30 A.M.: Light breakfast

ONE-TIME ACTION STEPS

- Buy a journal
- Choose three nonfiction books to read

and reading novels. None of these activities, she acknowledged, were critically important. With that in mind, we helped her to design a ritual aimed at disengaging earlier in the evening. Because she enjoyed taking baths and found them deeply relaxing, she decided to make a bath her nightly pre-sleep ritual at 10:00 p.m. Afterward, around 10:30, she went downstairs to her kitchen and had a cup of chamomile tea.

Jody was a worrier and one of the obstacles to falling asleep was that she tended to ruminate about the day ahead. At 10:45 p.m., when she got into bed, the first thing we had her do was to open the journal that she had purchased and half-jokingly named "Catharsis." Jody spent the next ten to fifteen minutes writing down any issues that she had on her mind and any thoughts she had about how to deal with them. Having committed whatever she was worrying about to paper, she found that she could usually let it go for the night. The final step in her ritual was to read for fifteen or twenty minutes—nonfiction. When she became absorbed in a novel, it tended to draw her in and keep her awake. When she focused on a more difficult and demanding book, it made her feel tired. Once she turned out her light at 11:15, Jody consciously turned her thoughts to some event in her life that evoked positive, relaxed feelings.

The second part of Jody's ritual centered on waking up. We urged her to begin by moving her alarm clock far enough away from her bed that turning it off would require getting up. We also urged her to immediately turn on all of the lights in the room, in order to stimulate her body to wake up. Next, Jody put on exercise clothes and immediately took a brisk ten- to fifteen-minute walk outside, once again to expose herself to natural light and increase her alertness. (High fitness makes it possible to perform on less sleep. If time is an issue, substituting a half hour of cardiovascular exercise or strength training for a half hour of sleep is a great trade.) Finally, Jody committed to eating a very light breakfast. Like most night owls, she simply didn't feel hungry in the morning, but eating, even lightly, was critical to jump-starting her metabolism.

During the first two weeks after instituting her new ritual, Jody slipped several times and stayed up as late as 1:00 a.m. But after succeeding for several days at turning off her light at 11:15—and then sleeping an average of seven hours—her energy level and her mood improved dramatically. She also found it much easier to wake up in the mornings. While she hated taking a brisk morning walk at first, doing so eventually become the part of her ritual she most enjoyed. It not only proved to be energizing, but also gave her an opportunity to reflect quietly on the day ahead before events overtook her.

By the end of four weeks, Jody was a convert. Her lights were out by 11:15 most nights. Eventually, she found that she didn't even require an alarm clock to get up. More important, both her mood and her capacity to sustain attention throughout the day noticeably improved.

OUR DAILY PULSE

You need not be a medical resident—or work exceptionally long hours—for fatigue and insufficient recovery to influence your level of engagement and performance. Just as we cycle through levels of sleep at night, so our potential for engagement varies during our waking hours. The shifts of energy that we experience are tied to the ultradian rhythms that regulate physiological markers of alertness at 90- to 120-minute intervals. Unfortunately, many of us override these naturally occurring rhythms to the point that they no longer even penetrate conscious awareness. The demands of our everyday lives are so intense and so consuming that they distract our attention from the subtler internal signals telling us that we need recovery.

In the absence of any artificial interventions, our energy stores naturally ebb and flow at different times of the day. Somewhere around 3:00 or 4:00 p.m. we reach the lowest phase of both our ultradian and our circadian rhythms. The Japanese sleep researchers Yoichi Tsuji and Toshinori Kobayashi have termed this "the breaking point"—the period of the day when most of us feel the highest level of fatigue. The documented vulnerability to accidents is far higher in the mid-afternoon than at any other daytime period. This explains why, over the centuries, so many cultures intuitively institutionalized the sort of midafternoon nap that is increasingly disappearing in our 24/7 world.

NASA's Fatigue Counter Measures Program has found that a short nap of just forty minutes improved performance by an average of 34 percent and alertness by 100 percent. In another recent study by Harvard researchers, subjects whose performance on a series of tasks dropped by as much as 50 percent in the course of a day were able to completely restore their highest levels of performance after a one-hour nap in the early afternoon. Winston Churchill was among the world leaders who clearly understood the strategic value of naps:

> You must sleep some time between lunch and dinner and no halfway measures. Take off your clothes and get into bed. That's what I always do. Don't think you will be doing less work because you sleep during the day. That's a foolish notion held by people who have no imagination. You will accomplish more. You get two days in one—well, at least one and a half, I'm sure. When the war started, I had to sleep during the day because that was the only way I could cope with my responsibilities.

While this luxury is not available to most people in business today, brief periods of rest are critical to sustaining energy over long hours. Those among our clients who find a way to get real recovery breaks throughout the day—and best of all brief catnaps sometime in the afternoon—consistently report that they sustain high energy well into the evenings.

BRUCE R.: WORK-LIFE BALANCE

By his own admission, Bruce R. was a workaholic. A highly successful thirty-seven-year-old executive for a magazine publishing company, he regularly

BRUCE R.

Performance Barrier: Work-life balance
Desired Outcome: Time for family,
  improved mood

RITUAL

10:00 A.M.: Recovery break: shoeshine,
  Starbucks visit
12:00 NOON: Lunch & music at desk
 3:00 P.M.: Recovery break: deep breathing
 6:00–8:00 A.M. Saturday & 8:00–10:00 P.M.
 Sunday: Designated periods for office-
 related work

ONE-TIME ACTION STEPS

■ Have assistant schedule breaks into every
day

arrived at work at 7:00 a.m., ate lunch most days
at his desk, never left earlier than 7 p.m., and often
worked at home late into the evening. Bruce
prided himself on putting in longer hours than
any of his colleagues—as many as eighty a week.
He also acknowledged that his schedule was
beginning to take a toll on him and on his family.
His output hadn't diminished, but his long days
left him feeling racy and distracted and his sense
of resentment and edginess had noticeably
increased. He had three children, seven, four, and

two, and his wife had stopped working when their second child was born. Increasingly, Bruce told us, she complained that he was rarely available to the family. Bruce felt especially guilty about not being a more involved father. His own father had been a highly driven corporate executive who devoted very little time to his family, and Bruce felt that he had suffered from his father's absence. He came to us seeking help in finding more balance in his life, but he made it clear that he wasn't willing to sacrifice his performance in work that he loved.

Bruce was moved by the evidence that the world's best athletes all build highly structured recovery routines into their lives. If periodic disengagement had the potential to help him be more effective at work, he found that reassuring. Highly structured by nature, he was willing to experiment with building rituals of renewal. The key, we explained, was to find forms of recovery that truly helped him to change channels and disengage from his work.

When we asked Bruce what nonwork activities gave him a feeling of real relaxation, the first one that he thought of was getting his shoes shined. He worked in a midtown Manhattan high-rise, and there was a shoeshine parlor three blocks from his office. Bruce decided that three times a week he would get up from his desk at 10:00 a.m. and walk to the shoeshine parlor. He had a favorite shoeshine man there, a buoyant man in his seventies who told wonderful stories. Between the walk to the stand, the shoeshine itself and the entertaining conversation, Bruce found those twenty minutes to be almost pure pleasure. He didn't have enough shoes to justify a visit five days a week, so on Tuesdays and Thursdays, his break consisted instead of walking down ten flights of stairs to the Starbucks near his office and having his one cherished cup of coffee for the day.

For lunch, Bruce still preferred not to go out, but he agreed to set aside his work for fifteen or twenty minutes. A classical music aficionado, he decided to put on his Walkman and listen to Beethoven or Mozart while he ate. Bruce discovered yet another form of recovery during the time he spent with us: yoga and breathing. At 3:00 p.m., he closed the door to his office, took off his shoes, and went through his postures on the floor for ten minutes. He followed this with ten minutes of deep breathing. It took him four weeks to lock in these new rituals so that they began to exert a noticeable pull on him.

Over time, Bruce built two other recovery rituals into his life. The first was for weekends. He wasn't prepared to give up work altogether, but in order to give more of himself to his family, he limited weekend work to two short, specific periods of time. The first was early Saturday mornings from 6:00 to 8:00 a.m., usually before anyone else was up. This allowed him to focus on paperwork that he had found it difficult to get done at the office. By dealing with it Saturday morning, it didn't weigh on him throughout the weekend. Unless there was an emergency, Bruce decided not to work on business at all the rest of Saturday and throughout the day Sunday.

The second work period was from 8:00 to 10:00 p.m. on Sunday evenings after his children went to sleep. This gave him the opportunity to catch up on email that came in over the weekend and plan for the week ahead. Bruce was not perfect in any of his rituals. When he fell behind at work, or faced an anxiety-producing deadline, he sometimes skipped his scheduled breaks during the day or felt himself preoccupied with work during the weekend. But whenever that happened, he noticed that he invariably felt less positive, more tired by the end of the day and more compromised in his ability to connect with his family.

The final recovery ritual that Bruce built was specifically for travel. He spent a fair amount of time on airplanes and he had always found this part of his life stressful and energy depleting. After 9/11, it became more difficult than ever. In an effort to transform his experience and to give himself a positive source of recovery, Bruce began packing a book that he would read purely for pleasure. He permitted himself to read the book only when he was on an airplane. The result was that he began to enjoy travel in a way that he never had before. Flying became far less of a stress in his life.

RAISING THE BAR

Given the number of benefits that we derive even from moderate exercise, it seems extraordinary that the vast majority of Americans do almost none. The explanation is surprisingly simple. Building strength and endurance requires pushing past our comfort zones and experiencing discomfort. It takes time before the obvious benefits kick in, and most of us quit before that ever occurs.

Both strength and cardiovascular training have a powerful impact on health, on energy levels and on performance (see box). Ever since the publication of Kenneth Cooper's book *Aerobics* in the mid-1960s, conventional wisdom has held that the best way to build fitness is through sustained aerobic or steady-state training. Our own experience is that interval training is preferable to continuous exercise and stress. Interval training first emerged as a method for increasing both the speed and endurance of runners in Europe in the 1930s. It involves short-to-moderate periods of exertion alternated with short-to-moderate periods of rest or reduced effort. The underlying premise is that a greater amount of intense work can be accomplished if it is interspersed with periods of rest.

The typical recommended exercise protocol is twenty to thirty minutes of continuous exercise, three to five days a week, at 60 to 85 percent of maximum heart rate. More recently, however, in

THE LINK BETWEEN EXERCISE EXPOSURE AND PERFORMANCE

- DuPont reported a 47.5% reduction in absenteeism over a six-year period for participants in a corporate fitness program. They also found that such employees used 14% fewer disability days than nonparticipants—a total of nearly 12,000 fewer disability days overall.
- A study in the journal *Ergonomics* concluded that "Mental performance was significantly better in the physically fit than in the un-fit. Fit workers committed 27% fewer errors on tasks involving concentration and short-term memory as compared to un-fit workers."
- In a study of eighty executives over a nine-month period, those who worked out regularly improved their fitness by 22% and demonstrated a 70% improvement in their ability to make complex decisions as compared with nonexercisers.
- The Canadian Life Assurance Company found that 63% of participants in a fitness program reported being more physically relaxed, less tired and more patient during the workday. Some 47% reported being more alert, had better rapport with supervisors and co-workers and experienced a higher level of enjoyment a work.
- At Union Pacific Railroad, 75% of employees reported that regular exercise improved their concentration and overall productivity at work.

- General Motors found that employees who participated in a physical fitness program had a 50% reduction in job grievances and on-the-job accidents, and a 40% reduction in lost time.
- The Coors Brewing Company found that it got as much as a $6.15 return for every $1 invested in a corporate fitness program. Companies including Equitable Life Assurance, General Mills and Motorola have all reported at least a $3 return for every dollar invested.

a joint study conducted by Harvard and Columbia Universities, researchers found that a series of short doses of intense aerobic activity—each one sixty seconds or less—followed by complete aerobic recovery, had a profound positive impact on participants. In a period of just eight weeks, the subjects exhibited significant improvements in cardiovascular fitness, heart-rate variability and mood. They also evidenced stronger immune systems and lower diastolic blood pressure.

We believe in the value of interval training not just for its physical benefits, but also for its practical applicability in navigating the challenges that we face in everyday life. Interval training has long been at the heart of our training process. It can take many forms: sprinting, walking up stairs and down, bicycling and even weight lifting, so long as the effect is to rhythmically raise and lower heart rate.

**Interval training is a means by which
to build more energy capacity
and to tolerate more stress, but also to
teach the body to recover more efficiently.**

Both energy expenditure and energy recovery are active physiological processes. In our experience, any form of linear energy expenditure—physical, emotional, mental or spiritual—is suboptimal for performance and potentially destructive over time. Full engagement requires the capacity to respond quickly and flexibly to whatever demands we face in our lives, but also to shut down and restore equilibrium quickly and efficiently.

STRENGTH FOR LIFE

Strength training is every bit as important as cardiovascular training, in part because loss of physical strength is so connected with the markers of aging and with reduced energy capacity. On average, we lose nearly one-half pound of muscle mass per year after the age of forty in the absence of regular strength training. Since the mid-1980s, researchers at Tufts University have produced extraordinary data about the effects of strength training among the elderly. In a study published in the *Journal of American Medical Association* in 1990, for example, a group of nursing home residents ages eighty-six to ninety-six underwent a strength-training program. All of them had serious chronic diseases and most of them used walkers or canes. After training just three days a week for eight weeks, the subjects increased their average strength by 175 percent and their balance by 48 percent.

More recently, one of the Tufts researchers, Miriam Nelson, launched a controlled study of women aged fifty-five to seventy who had previously done no exercise at all. After a year, those who continued not to exercise lost 2 percent of their bone density and suffered an 8.5 percent loss of balance. Those who undertook a three-day-a-week strength-training program gained 1 percent in bone density and 14 percent in balance. More broadly, strength training has also been shown to increase overall energy, speed metabolism and strengthen the heart.

The growing consensus among physiologists is that muscle loss, more than any single factor, is responsible for both the frailty and the diminished vitality associated with old age. Loss of bone density, for example, vastly increases the incidence of osteoporosis, which makes the bones far more fragile and affects some 25 million Americans. By the age of ninety, one in three women will have suffered a fracture of the hip. Remarkably, more women die as a consequence of hip fractures than from breast cancer, uterine cancer and ovarian cancer combined.

Building physical energy capacity is sometimes referred to as "toughening." In the largely sedentary world of white-collar workers, the absence of any regular physical demand precludes the natural toughening that occurs simply from a physically active life. The result is that as we age, most of us have less energy available to cope with challenging and stressful situations.

A long-term study of soldiers who participated in one of the most intensive training programs in the armed forces clearly supports this conclusion. The study included some two hundred soldiers who underwent the Survival, Evasion, Resistance and Escape Course, or SERE, taught at Fort Bragg's JFK Special Warfare Center and School— one of the most rigorous and stressful trainings offered in any branch of the military.

The SERE participants were compared with soldiers undergoing other forms of training, as well as pilots performing military flight operations, novice skydivers making their first jump and civilian patients about to undergo major surgery. All subjects provided saliva samples, so that their stress hormone levels could be assessed before, during and after the demanding event. The study found that the SERE soldiers consistently recovered more quickly than others from a given stressful event, and in turn were better prepared to meet the next challenge. The key factor appeared to be the SERE method of exposing subjects to intense stress offset by intermittent recovery. As authors C. A. Morgan III and Major Gary Hazlett concluded:

Rigorous training improves a person's ability to perform on the battlefield. . . . The concept of stress inoculation is very much like the concept of preventing a particular disease through vaccination. Like immunization, which occurs only when the vaccine is given in the proper dosage, stress inoculation occurs only when the stress intensity is at the optimal level—high enough to activate a person's psychological and biological systems, but low enough so as not to overwhelm them. If the stress level is not high enough, inoculation will not occur; if the stress level is too high, stress sensitization will occur, and the individual will probably perform less effectively when he is stressed again.

In short, minimizing or avoiding stress is just as destructive to capacity as excessive stress without recovery. In a study published in the medical journal *Lancet*, researchers looked at the effects of bed rest on some 16,000 patients with fifteen different medical problems. It turned out that patients got no significant beneficial effect from prolonged bed rest, regardless of their medical condition. To the contrary, bed rest tended to delay recovery and in some cases cause further damage to the patient. These conclusions even applied to conditions for which bed rest has long been recommended, including low back pain, recovery after a heart attack and acute infectious hepatitis.

FRANK K.: LOW STRESS TOLERANCE

The primary performance barrier that showed up on Frank K.'s Full Engagement Inventory was low stress tolerance—a tendency to become easily frustrated and harsh with others when under pressure. As a newly promoted department head for a large retailer that was struggling, Frank was frequently critical and often lost his temper with his colleagues. Despite his immense talent, he was not operating at his best—and his feedback from his direct reports confirmed that conclusion.

Frank had an aversion to exercise. At the age of forty-six, he was perhaps twenty pounds overweight, but he still had more energy than most of the younger people he supervised. He understood that exercise would serve his health and periodically, under pressure from his wife, he halfheartedly took up jogging. The problem was that a blend of boredom and discomfort inevitably prompted him to give up within a couple of weeks.

Our promise to Frank was that building regular exercise into his life would prove to be one powerful way to release his tension and get his emotions under better control. We also pointed out that he had never stuck with an exercise program long enough to derive any benefits. Skeptically but gamely, Frank committed to an exercise program for sixty days—the outer limit of what it typically takes to put a new ritual into

FRANK K.

Performance Barrier: Low stress tolerance
Desired Outcome: Calmness, self-control

RITUAL

Monday 7:00 A.M.: Walking
Wednesday 6:30 A.M.: Walking, strength
training
Friday 7:00 A.M.: Walking/jogging
Sunday 11:00 A.M.: Interval training,
strength training

ONE-TIME ACTION STEPS

▪ Buy a heart-rate monitor
▪ Buy new workout clothes

place. He also signed up for a two-month membership at his local health club.

Next, we helped Frank to design an interval-based exercise program. The key to any new fitness regimen is to start slowly and build incrementally. We suggested that Frank purchase a heart-rate monitor as a way to measure precisely his stress-recovery patterns. Given his age and his lack of previous exercise, he set 140 beats a minute as his target heart rate. (Check with your physician before selecting your own target rate.) At first, Frank found that he could reach that rate simply by walking fast. He maintained it for sixty seconds and then slowed down until his heart rate dropped to 90. He repeated the same up-and-down sequence for the next twenty minutes. Rather than pushing himself continuously for twenty or twenty-five minutes, he was teaching his body both to tolerate stress and to recover efficiently.

Almost immediately, Frank discovered that working in intervals was more absorbing and more compelling than his previous attempts at jogging. He felt moderately pushed during his new work-outs, but not to the point that he was tempted to quit. The second week, he began to experiment with different intervals on alternate days. On one day he moved in a narrower range between 100 and 130 heartbeats a minute. In the next session he oscillated between 100 and 140. Over time, he began jogging to reach the targeted rate.

Initially, Frank committed to three mornings a week—Monday, Wednesday and Friday at 7:00 a.m. He chose those times on the grounds that if he didn't get his exercise early, he was far less likely to do it at all. He also committed to strength training twice a week. Strength training is intrinsically a form of interval training—lifting a weight a certain number of repetitions and then resting. The most basic workout is exercising each of the six major body parts—shoulders, back, chest, biceps, triceps and legs—by doing a single set of eight to twelve repetitions for each body part at an appropriate weight. Once again, our goal was to get Frank to expose himself incrementally to challenge, but not to so much that he would feel sore, exhausted and tempted to quit.

In his fourth week, Frank had to meet a series of deadlines at work and he skipped three consecutive days of exercise. To his surprise, he actually missed exercising, and decided to go to his health club the following Sunday morning even though it wasn't scheduled. On a whim, he took a spinning class and found that he loved it. Spinning is built around intervals—increasing and decreasing the tension and speed on a stationary bike while listening to music. Frank discovered that he could handle the challenge surprisingly well and that he enjoyed the camaraderie of his fellow spinners. He decided to add the Sunday class to his weekly regimen, and to build in a strength-training workout afterwards.

Frank's thirteen-year-old son loved bicycle riding, and as the weather got warmer, Frank suggested one Saturday morning that they take a ride together. They ended up bicycling ten miles to a nearby town, having breakfast together and then riding back. It dawned on Frank that this was a terrific way to spend time with his son, and he suggested that they do it again the following week. Without any forethought, it quickly became their Saturday morning routine and proved to be a precious time together for each of them.

By the end of eight weeks, Frank had locked in a five-day-a-week exercise ritual that had largely acquired a life of its own. Much as we promised, it became an effective source of mental and emotional recovery, and he felt palpably less edgy at work. Because he also had more energy, he was able to get more done during the day and to feel less pressed in the evening.

BEAR IN MIND

- Physical energy is the fundamental source of fuel in life.
- Physical energy is derived from the interaction between oxygen and glucose.
- The two most important regulators of physical energy are breathing and eating.
- Eating five to six low-calorie, highly nutritious meals a day ensures a steady resupply of glucose and essential nutrients.
- Drinking sixty-four ounces of water daily is a key factor in the effective management of physical energy.
- Most human beings require seven to eight hours of sleep per night to function optimally.
- Going to bed early and waking up early help to optimize performance.
- Interval training is more effective than steady-state exercise in building physical capacity and in teaching people how to recover more efficiently.
- To sustain full engagement, we must take a recovery break every 90 to 120 minutes.

CHAPTER 5

EMOTIONAL ENERGY:
TRANSFORMING THREAT
INTO CHALLENGE

Physical energy is the raw fuel for igniting our emotional skills and talents. In order to perform at our best we must access pleasant and positive emotions: enjoyment, challenge, adventure and opportunity. Emotions that arise out of threat or deficit—fear, frustration, anger, sadness—have a decidedly toxic feel to them and are associated with the release of specific stress hormones, most notably cortisol. From our perspective, emotional intelligence is simply the capacity to manage emotions skillfully in the service of high positive energy and full engagement. In practical terms, the key "muscles" or competencies that fuel positive emotion are self-confidence, self-control (self-regulation), social skills (interpersonal effectiveness) and empathy. Smaller, supportive "muscles" include patience, openness, trust and enjoyment.

Access to the emotional muscles that best serve performance depends on creating a balance between exercising them regularly and intermittently seeking recovery. Much the way that we deplete cardiovascular capacity or exhaust a bicep by exposing it to stress, so we run down emotionally if we are constantly spending emotional energy without recovery. When our emotional muscles are weak or insufficient to meet demand—if we have a lack of confidence or too little patience, for example—we must systematically build capacity by devising rituals to push past our current capacity and then recover.

Physical and emotional energy capacity are inextricably connected. When demand begins to deplete our physical energy reserves, one of the consequences is that we begin to feel a sense of emergency. We move into the high negative energy quadrant, which alerts us that some need isn't being met. This was precisely what had happened in Roger B.'s life. Because he paid so little attention to renewing physical energy, the quantity of fuel in his tank had diminished over time. At the same time, he perceived that the pressures and demands in his life were increasing inexorably. Feeling neglected by his boss, worried about his job and disconnected from his family, Roger became increasingly dominated by the experience of anxiety, frustration and defensiveness.

From an energy perspective, negative emotions are costly and inefficient. Much like a gas-guzzling car, they draw down our energy stores at a rapid rate. For leaders and managers, negative emotions are doubly insidious, because they are so infectious. If we are prompting fear, anger and defensiveness in others, we progressively undermine their ability to perform effectively. Chronic negative emotions—most especially anger and depression—have also been correlated with a broad range of disorders and diseases ranging from back pain and headaches to heart disease and cancer.

Epidemiologist David Snowdon made precisely this correlation in his study of 678 aging nuns in the School Sisters of Notre Dame Congregation. Snowden set out to study the factors that differentiate nuns who eventually got Alzheimer's disease from those who did not. All of the nuns he studied had been required to write a personal essay when they came into the order in their early twenties. Upon analysis, Snowden discovered that those nuns whose writing expressed a preponderance of positive emotions (happiness, love, hope, gratitude and contentment) tended to live longer and more productive lives. Nuns with the highest number of positive-emotion sentences had half the risk of death at any age as those with the lowest number of such sentences. This is consistent with the findings from several other studies suggesting that a history of depression—the most insidious of all negative emotions—increases twofold the likelihood of eventually developing Alzheimer's. These findings deeply influenced Snowdon not just professionally, but also personally. "I now [make] a conscious effort to regain my physiological balance quickly after an upset," he explains. "I try not to stay stuck in negativity. My goal is to return my body to its normal, healthier state as soon as possible."

In Roger's case, he had yet to experience any significant health problems, although he had noticed an increasing pattern of headaches and nagging back pain that distracted and sometimes preoccupied him. As he got into his work with us, Roger started to see other ways in which his negative energy had taken a toll in his life. On days that he felt especially anxious, he noticed that his focus and perseverance failed. When his impatience rose, his interactions with his colleagues became edgier, and he seemed to get less accomplished. Whenever he felt consumed by frustration, a racy sort of exhaustion set in by midday, which left him feeling drained of motivation to work. On those increasingly rare days when he felt relaxed and in control, Roger was able to stay positively engaged no matter how many demands he was facing.

The impact of negative emotions on performance is especially clear in sports. Consider for a moment the contrast between the careers of two tennis greats—John McEnroe and Jimmy Connors. Throughout his career, the volatile McEnroe was easily provoked to anger and frustration by his own mistakes or by line calls that he didn't like. Connors was similarly volatile early in his career, but as he grew older and more experienced, he began to play with an increasing sense of joy, playfulness, and passion. McEnroe, by contrast, seemed to get very little enjoyment from playing, and his outbursts grew worse as he got older. Connors derived his energy from a sense of opportunity and adventure, while McEnroe's came more from a defensive posture. He always seemed to be fighting for his life.

On one level, McEnroe's negativity didn't appear to affect his performance. Connors may have had more fun, but both players managed to achieve the number one ranking in the world for several years consecutively, and both won numerous Grand Slams. So what then is the evidence that positive emotion is a better fuel for performance? The answer is endurance. On his thirty-ninth birthday, Connors, arguably the less gifted of the two players, reached the semifinals of the U.S. Open. He didn't retire from the tour until the age of forty. McEnroe retired six years sooner, at the age of thirty-four. At the most basic level, Connors managed his emotional energy far more efficiently than did McEnroe, and was able to play at a high level for far longer. He also got a lot more enjoyment along the way.

Today, McEnroe himself recognizes some of the costs of playing matches in the high negative quadrant. Comparing himself to other players who better controlled their emotions, he writes: "My shtick, of course, was getting upset. Did it help me more than hurt me? I don't think so. Ultimately, my father was right—I probably would have done better if I hadn't ever gotten into that. But I could never rest on my talent or on anything." McEnroe's inability to control his anger, he now believes, was a key factor in what he calls "the worst loss of my life, a devastating defeat"—to Ivan Lendl in the finals of the French Open in 1984, after being up two sets to none. "I wasted too much energy at the French by getting angry," he explained in his recent autobiography. The experience briefly gave him religion, and he brought this new understanding to his next tournament—Wimbledon. "From the first match at the All England Club," he says, "I was determined not to do anything that would derail me from avenging Roland Garros (site of the French Open)." Sure enough, McEnroe won Wimbledon, and, not coincidentally, he controlled his temper throughout the tournament.

If positive emotion more efficiently fuels individual high performance, it also has a profound organizational impact. After interviewing a large sample of managers and their employees, the Gallup Organization found that no single factor more clearly predicts the productivity of an employee than his relationship with his direct superior. More specifically, Gallup found that the key drivers of productivity for employees include whether they feel cared for by a supervisor or someone at work; whether they have received recognition or praise during the past seven days; and whether someone at work regularly encourages their development. Put another way, the ability to communicate consistently positive energy lies at the heart of effective management.

For many years, Roger B. himself was motivated at work in significant part by the feeling that his boss cared for and believed in him. With a supportive wind at his back, he grew more confident of his own value, more positive in his approach to others, and ultimately more successful as a salesman. Success tends to feed on itself, reinforcing the positive emotions that fuel performance in the first place. The reverse is also true. When his boss became less available and less visibly supportive, Roger's enjoyment and sense of security at work diminished, and so, too, did his confidence, his level of engagement and, ultimately, his performance.

As his own emotional energy turned more negative, Roger began to have the same demoralizing impact on his direct reports that his boss's lack of attention had on him. Stop for a moment and think about someone who has been a mentor in your life. Was his or her energy positive or negative? Have you been more motivated and inspired in your life when you were encouraged, supported and challenged or when you were criticized, judged and threatened?

ENJOYMENT AND RENEWAL

Simply changing channels is an effective method to refuel emotionally. During the past decade, we have been surprised and dismayed to discover how infrequently most people undertake activities simply because they are enjoyable and emotionally nourishing. One of the most revealing questions that we ask the clients who come through our training is how frequently in their lives they experience a sense of joy or deep satisfaction. The most common answer we get is "rarely." Think for a moment about your own life. How many hours a week do you devote to activities purely for the pleasure and renewal they provide? What percentage of the time would you describe yourself as feeling deeply relaxed? When was the last time you truly let go and felt fully disconnected?

Any activity that is enjoyable, fulfilling and affirming tends to prompt positive emotions. Depending on your interests, that may mean singing, gardening, dancing, making love, doing yoga, reading an absorbing book, playing a sport, visiting a museum, attending a concert, or simply spending quiet, reflective time alone after an intense day of engaging with other people. The key, we have found, is making such activities priorities, and treating the time that you invest in them as sacrosanct. The point is not just that pleasure is its own reward, but more practically, that it is a critical ingredient in sustained performance.

The depth or quality of emotional renewal is something else again. That depends on how absorbing, enriching and enlivening the activity turns out to be. Television, for example, is one of the primary means by which most people relax and recover. For the most part, however, watching television is the mental and emotional equivalent of eating junk food. It may provide a temporary form of recovery, but it is rarely nutritious and it is easy to consume too much. Researchers such as Mihaly Csikszentmihalyi have found that prolonged television watching is actually correlated with increased anxiety and low-level depression. Conversely, the richer and deeper the source of emotional recovery, the more we refill our reserves and the more resilient we become. Effective emotional renewal puts us in a position to perform more effectively, especially under pressure.

ERICA R.: ANXIETY, RIGIDITY

Erica R. was a highly successful lawyer at a large corporate firm. Her complaint was that she felt relentlessly pressured by the demands of her job, forever worried about the quality of her work and guilty about giving too little time to her two sons, ages eleven and thirteen. Life struck her as an unending series of obligations, and she took every one of them seriously. To control her anxiety, Erica planned her time meticulously and held herself to exacting standards. She had a reputation for being very good at what she did but also for being rigid and brusque with people. Her relationship with her partners was respectful but distant, and many of the firm's associates tried to avoid being assigned to cases with her.

The issue for Erica was less about increasing capacity than it was about relaxing and letting go. Like many of our clients—especially women—she took almost no time for herself. When we asked her to recall a time of great joy in her life, she thought first about the birth of her two children. The only other memories that came immediately to mind were the night of her high school prom and the day of her marriage. Not one of these events had occurred less than a decade ago. Just thinking about taking time for pleasure and relaxation, Erica sheepishly acknowledged, made her feel uncomfortable. Even on vacations with her family, she played the role of chief tour guide, determined to see as many sights as possible and unable to contemplate lying on a beach and simply relaxing.

We suggested to Erica that she could be more effective at work, personally and interpersonally, if she created more space between obligations and took specific time out to simply enjoy herself and to refuel emotionally. She already had in place a very regular early-morning exercise regimen, but it was scarcely a source of pleasure. She went to the gym four days a week before work, and pushed

ERICA R.

Targeted Muscle: Flexibility
Performance Barrier: Anxiety, rigidity
Desired Outcome: Enjoyment, balance

RITUAL

Mon, Wed, Fri: Lunch in the arboretum
Tuesdays: Dance class at lunch
9:00–11:00 A.M. Saturdays: Gardening

ONE-TIME ACTION STEPS

■ Sign up for dance classes
■ Choose three novels to read

herself relentlessly for thirty to forty minutes on the step machine or the treadmill. She found exercise monotonous, and she hated having to wake up so early in order to get back home before her children awoke. It was just one more obligation to get through.

We asked Erica if there was any form of physical activity that she genuinely enjoyed. As a child, she told us, she had been a dancer, and while she had finally burned out on the rigorous demands of ballet, she had always loved other forms of dance such as modern, jazz and African. We suggested that she substitute dance classes for her workouts at least a couple of days a week, and consider taking them at the end of the day before returning home as a way to make the transition. Erica agreed to give it a shot. In a short time, dance classes became simultaneously a source of pleasure, a means to fully disconnect from work, and something to which she found herself eagerly looking forward.

As we explored further, Erica told us that a second great love in her youth had been reading fiction. As an adult, however, she rarely read for pleasure at all. Spending time in nature was the other activity that she had experienced as deeply renewing but rarely found time to do. Erica decided to devise a ritual that combined both sources of enjoyment. Even though she lived in a warm climate, she had for years eaten lunch at her desk in order to save time. She decided to create a forty-five minute routine around taking a bag lunch to an arboretum five minutes from her office and eating on a bench while reading a novel. In addition, on Saturday mornings she set aside two hours for gardening.

At first, Erica told us, these new routines seemed almost intolerably indulgent—akin to cutting a class in school. But the blend of dance classes, gardening and her time in the park made her feel so much better in such a short time that all three activities began to exert a strong pull on her. The impact cascaded into her professional life. Rather than feeling resentful about her workload, as she had for several years, she found that she was able to rediscover a good deal of satisfaction in the intellectual challenge it provided. She remained a demanding taskmasker, but she began to see that she could also serve as a mentor to associates. She also saw that when she was more encouraging, she was often more effective. In the evenings—most especially after dance class—she began to be able to relax more with her husband and children. On the days that Erica didn't dance or take her lunch in the park, she could feel a palpable difference both in her anxiety level and in her ability to focus in the afternoons.

HEALING IN THE BROKEN PLACES

In some instances, we face involuntary emotional storms—challenges that come to us unbidden. Depending on how we manage them, they can either overwhelm us or serve as an opportunity for growth. It is hard to imagine a more severe test of emotional capacity than to have been working at the World Trade Center on the morning of September 11, 2001. Jeffrey S. is a longtime client of ours and a managing director at a financial services firm headquartered directly across the street from the Twin Towers. When the first plane hit, Jeffrey watched in horror from his forty-sixth-floor window. Two of his largest accounts were companies headquartered in the two buildings. As Jeffrey helped to supervise the evacuation of his own firm's employees, he realized in horror that dozens of friends and colleagues were likely trapped in the two burning buildings next door. He was two blocks away when the first tower collapsed, and he ended up walking seven miles uptown to get home. When he finally reunited with his wife and his ten-month-old daughter, he collapsed in tears. "I just completely lost it," he told us.

In the weeks ahead, Jeffrey struggled to regain his footing. Accustomed to working out every day, he found it hard at first to summon any motivation to continue. In a short time, however, he realized that keeping this physical routine helped anchor him to a sense of normalcy and provided a source of emotional recovery each day. Given the pressures he was under, it dawned on Jeffrey that he actually needed more energy capacity than usual. Difficult as it was, he decided to increase the intensity of his workouts. He also committed himself to playing with his young daughter every night, even when he was feeling exhausted and depressed. On one level, that meant putting aside his own seemingly urgent needs. On another, he derived a powerful source of renewal from his time with his child. Perhaps the most extraordinary and unexpected dimension of Jeffrey's experience grew out of dealing with the deaths of so many friends and colleagues. For three months after September 11, he attended at least one and sometimes as many as two or three funerals and memorial services a week—several dozen in all, nearly all for people in their twenties and thirties. It was painful, fiercely sad, and exhausting, but at a certain point it dawned on Jeffrey that it was also enormously healing and deepening.

"In a way these funerals made it more difficult to get back to a normal life," Jeffrey told us. "But what happened is that I found myself converting them into an opportunity to honor and pay tribute to all of these people who had been so important to me. It was also a chance to be with other people who were going through the same things I was. These services gave me a chance to express my deep feelings to the families of the people I had known. Many of the funerals became a celebration of life. It was more than a humbling experience, it was leveling, but I think I got stronger for it, in part because I took more time for recovery.

"The grief still comes in waves, but I feel clearer than ever about my priorities. Some people in our office were so traumatized that they never came back to work after September 11. I had been training at LGE for years, learning how to balance stress and recovery, but really it was just to be better, to exceed myself. Now I realize that there are a couple of times in your life that really matter, pivotal moments when what you've got to draw on makes all the difference in how you emerge from the darkness. This was one of them."

RELATIONSHIPS AS STRESS RENEWAL

Creating a rhythmic balance between energy expenditure and energy recovery is more complex emotionally than it is physically, but no less critical to optimal performance and full engagement. The delicate dance of a healthy friendship, for example, can be a powerful source both of positive energy and of renewal. Gallup found that one of the key factors in sustained performance is having at least one good friend at work. The pulse of a strong relationship involves a rhythmic movement between giving and taking, talking and listening, valuing the other person and feeling commensurately valued in return. A relationship in which you do most of the giving and receive very little in return ultimately prompts a sense of deficit and emptiness. A self-absorbed relationship isn't really much of a relationship at all.

When Barbara P. came to see us, she was a single, thirty-seven-year-old marketing executive who worked exceptionally long hours at her job, in part because she had few friends or outside interests. She ended most days feeling exhausted, resentful and even despairing. After going through our program, and confronting her performance barriers, Barbara recognized that one key to feeling better was to systematically build more recovery into her life. She began by taking an aerobics class at a nearby health club after work each day. As we have noted, a challenging physical workout often serves as a source of positive emotional renewal. Sure enough, Barbara invariably finished her workouts feeling more positive. As she became more physically fit, she felt better about herself and better equipped to handle demands and deal with setbacks at work.

To her surprise, the most powerful source of positive renewal for Barbara came from the relationships that she made along the way. The aerobics class provided a way to connect with others, and she began to go out regularly for dinner with several of her classmates. Where she had long felt isolated and unappreciated at work, Barbara found that she was able to relax, laugh and talk freely with her new friends. She became as invested in their lives as they did in hers. Nourished and renewed by the time with these new friends, she built a reservoir of positive emotional energy that she could draw from at her job. Because she was in a more upbeat mood when she arrived at work in the mornings, she found that she was often able to concentrate better. She also became less reactive and more relaxed in her dealings with colleagues and her boss, and her professional relationships improved. When she worked too long without breaks, she could still lose her temper or turn negative, which set her back. But on balance her more positive feelings fed on one another. Barbara found herself spending so much less energy on anger, resentment and frustration that she was more able to engage positively at work.

JED R.: LACK OF DEPTH IN RELATIONSHIPS

Jed R.'s issue wasn't so much the absence of other relationships in his life, but the fact that he gave them so little time and energy. At the age of forty-eight, he was the head of creative services for a midsize advertising agency. Charming and quick-witted, he was well-liked and highly successful, but he also felt increasingly detached and restless at work, as if he were just going through the motions. The biggest void in his life, he told us, was the quality of his relationships. Whether it was with colleagues and direct reports at the office or with his wife and child at home, he felt that his connections were disturbingly thin and superficial. Jed feared that his wife's complaints about his unavailability were beginning to threaten their marriage. They had one child, an eleven-year-old girl, and he worried that he was distant from her, too. At work, he had perfectly pleasant relationships with his colleagues and direct reports, but he felt very little depth of connection with any of them.

Jed decided to build a series of rituals around investing more time and energy in the key people in his life. He began with his wife, suggesting that they set aside ninety minutes on Saturday mornings just to talk and catch up on the week. He also suggested that they build in a date night every other week on Wednesday evenings, and that on

JED R.

Targeted Muscle: Intimacy

Performance Barrier: Lack of depth in relationships

Desired Outcome: Deeper connections with others

RITUAL

Monday evenings: Dinner with daughter

Alternate Wednesdays: Date night with wife

8:00–9:30 A.M. Saturdays: Quiet time to talk with wife

1:00–2:00 P.M. Fridays: Lunch with direct report

6:00 P.M. first Monday of each month: Staff event

those weeks when either of them had to travel, they try to reschedule the date for the following week.

Jed also established a weekly Monday night dinner out with his daughter. Doing so gave his wife an opportunity to take a web-design class at a local community college. Jed quickly discovered that he derived great pleasure from the time alone with his daughter, and she clearly valued and looked forward to their time together as well. Much like Rachel P., Jed found that the positive energy he derived from the time with his wife and with his child gave him an increased sense of buoyancy and energy on the job.

At work, Jed decided to institute a lunch each Friday with one of his direct reports. He sensed their apprehension at first, since they were unused to so much attention, but word soon got around that he had no particular agenda. Jed grew more connected with his direct reports, and several of them went out of their way to tell him how much they appreciated his willingness to take time for them. Several months later, Jed decided to build a second ritual at work. Once every other month, at the end of the workday, he invited his staff to join together for an activity—bowling, or dinner, or ice-skating. It was a chance to spend time together in an informal setting. Consciously and systematically devoting more time and energy to his family and to his colleagues left Jed feeling more connected at home and more invested in his work.

EXPANDING EMOTIONAL CAPACITY

There are times when demand overwhelms our emotional capacity, even if we are regularly seeking renewal. Just as there is only so much weight you can lift without running up against your limits, so there is only so much emotional demand you can tolerate without turning negative. The best way to build an emotional muscle, much like a physical

JUDITH F.

Targeted Muscle: Confidence
Performance Barrier: Insecurity and low
  self-esteem
Desired Outcome: Expand business, trust
  instincts

RITUAL

9:00 A.M. Mondays, Wednesdays: At least
  one follow-up call to a professional lead
2:00–4:00 P.M. Fridays: Language tutoring
Give all clients genuine feedback on design
  issues

muscle, is to push past your current comfort zone and then recover.

Perhaps no obstacle to full engagement and high performance is so pervasive and so vexing as insecurity and low self-esteem. Complex and subtle factors account for such feelings, but positive energy rituals can nonetheless be effective in building greater self-confidence. Judith F. had a reasonably successful design business, but lived in constant fear that she would one day be revealed as the imposter she felt herself to be. Anyone who really knew her couldn't possibly like her, she believed. As a result, she was reluctant to actively reach out for new clients and instead relied exclusively on word-of-mouth referrals. She was also reluctant to say what she really felt with clients who had strong opinions of their own for fear of antagonizing them. The cost was that she often felt inauthentic and she sometimes failed to give clients the benefit of her very well developed and sophisticated design sense.

We began by helping Judith to shift her equation from worrying about how others viewed her to focusing on living each day guided by her own deepest values. The two values that she identified as most fundamental were genuineness and courage, neither of which she felt she exemplified in her everyday life. For years, she would meet people in her community or through her work and see an opportunity to pursue them as potential clients. Fearful of rejection, she wouldn't follow up. One of the first rituals Judith created was to set a quota of calls that she would make to reach out to people—designating Monday and Wednesday mornings at 9:00 a.m. to pursue new professional leads.

In a paradigm shift, Judith increasingly began to measure herself by the courage she demonstrated in making these weekly calls and not by the particular response she received. She also committed to telling every client who hired her what she really thought about any significant design issue that came up, even if it meant disagreeing with them.

Simultaneously, Judith made a decision to be more genuine with people in her personal life rather than trying to figure out how to please them, as she had done in the past. To her surprise and relief, the responses she got, both personally and professionally, were far more positive than she anticipated. Most of her clients especially appreciated her clarity and definitiveness. Her old insecurities didn't simply disappear. When she encountered an especially difficult client, she found herself reverting to her old inclination to defer and simply go along in order not to rock the boat. Over time, however, Judith found that she became less concerned with how people viewed her, and began deriving a sense of accomplishment and strength instead from having acted consistently with the values she held most dear. She discovered that it was possible to be tactful without being inauthentic.

The second ritual Judith instituted was to devote some of her time to a cause that she cared about. Giving to others, she decided, was an investment of her time and energy that she very much wanted to make. The activity she chose gave her the opportunity to draw on a strength she had not tapped for many years. Judith had a gift for languages, and she spoke French and Spanish fluently. It turned out that a public high school in the town adjacent to hers had a large population of Spanish-speaking students with a great need for remedial help in learning English. Judith volunteered her time one afternoon a week and got some very precious benefits in return: the opportunity to feel both competent and useful, and a sense of genuine appreciation from the school administrators and from many of the kids as well. While her purpose in volunteering was not to improve her performance at work, the positive ways that it made her feel about herself spilled over into the rest of her life. This was true not just when it came to seeking new clients, but also in the confidence she brought to her design work itself.

ALAN D.: POOR LISTENING SKILLS, LOW EMPATHY

One of the primary barriers our clients face in the workplace is difficulty getting along with bosses and colleagues. Likewise, one of the key challenges for leaders and managers is creating positive relationships with their direct reports.

Alan D. was the head of the marketing division of a large consumer-products company. Valued for his quick, penetrating mind and his immense creativity, he tended to dominate any project in which he got involved. In Alan's mind, he was simply trying to get the best result. The problem was that he frequently left his colleagues and direct reports feeling unvalued, unheard and even demeaned. Alan was dismayed to discover, through his Full Engagement Inventory data, that while he was appreciated for his brilliance and creativity, he was also viewed as distant, uncommunicative and critical. His immediate instinct was to attribute this feedback to the high standard that he set. He had

ALAN D.

Targeted Muscle: Empathy

Performance Barrier: Poor listening skills, low empathy

Desired Outcome: Deeper relationships

RITUAL

2:00 P.M.: Visit with an employee

Begin interactions by listening, not by speaking

Reflect back to the speaker what I think I heard, using my own words

Use phrases such as "I think I understand what you are saying"

the same explanation for the high turnover in his department. He also told us that he didn't consider it an efficient use of his time to "hang out" with employees. As we probed a little deeper, Alan acknowledged that he was uncomfortable with intimacy and awkward at small talk. It also dawned on him, for the first time, that he almost never focused on how others might be feeling as he entered a collaborative venture.

While some people are simply more hard-wired than others for specific emotional competencies, that doesn't preclude developing a given emotional muscle to the limits of its potential. Empathy simply wasn't in Alan's emotional vocabulary. To build this muscle—to learn to experience the world from a wholly different perspective than his own—required practice and repetition. We appealed first to Alan's sense of logic. Until he really learned how to listen to others without interruption and instant judgment, we suggested, how could he fairly judge their competence? If his behavior made people feel that he wasn't truly listening to them, we said, then how likely were they to feel motivated by him or to produce their best and most creative work?

True empathy requires letting go of our own agendas, at least temporarily.

Alan decided to build a ritual focused on listening more attentively and trying to put himself in the shoes of the person with whom he was talking. Rather than rushing in with his own point of view, he committed to beginning meetings by listening to others in a structured way—intermittently reflecting back in his own words what he had just heard without critiquing it. Alan found it revelatory to discover that he didn't necessarily have to agree with what another person was saying in order to respectfully acknowledge a different point of view. He did this by using phrases such as "I can see why that makes sense" and "I understand how what I said might make you feel that." When it came time to express his own opinion, he chose phrasings such as "Let me suggest another way of looking at this," or "I wonder if there is a possibility of taking another approach." He also tried to lower his voice when he spoke. His goal was to stay attentive to how what he said was likely to affect the energy of others in the room.

These sorts of fundamental changes in personal style are very difficult to make, and Alan struggled with them during the weeks after he first built his ritual. Our experience—and considerable research—suggests that setbacks are an intrinsic part of any significant change process. The motivation to make a change, and even the specific plan for doing so, may often just be the first step. The researcher James Prochaska has found, for example, that people launching a major change in their lives often fail several times before succeeding in a sustaining way.

Because Alan's ritual felt awkward to him at first, he used it very selectively. By the end of a month, however, he noticed that when he was more affirmative—nodding his head when he listened, paraphrasing what he had heard—it had a palpably positive impact on others. Often he could see their body language change. They sat up straighter, leaned forward in their chairs, became more alive and animated. Alan was also fascinated to discover that the nature of his interchanges with people changed. The more that he was able to listen attentively, the freer people became about offering their own ideas and the more he began to see that his own point of view wasn't always necessarily complete—or even accurate.

Alan also decided to institute a routine of getting up from his desk in the afternoons in order to visit the offices of one of his direct reports. At first, it felt awkward and he limited himself to very small time increments—three or four minutes, which seemed tolerable. He also talked strictly about business issues. Even at that, however, Alan could sense that the colleagues he stopped in to see were very happy to have his undivided attention. Their appreciation made him feel more relaxed, and over the next several months he extended his visits to ten or fifteen minutes. For Alan himself, these sessions became a source of recovery—a means of switching channels after intense periods of work at his desk. He also noticed that several of his top executives began showing up at his office door more frequently to discuss issues, rather than emailing him, as they had always done previously.

While Alan had spent years in a collaborative business, he found that systematically building the capacity to listen attentively and to connect more personally with colleagues opened him for the first time to the depth, richness and excitement of other points of view. He recognized that he still had a good distance to travel, but he felt that he had already become a significantly more effective and inspiring leader.

PAUL M.: IMPATIENT, OVERLY CRITICAL

Paul M. made no bones about the fact that he was impatient, easily irritated and highly demanding of the employees in the health club company that he ran. "It helps me to get more things done and it's who I am," he told us. "I just consider myself very direct and very results-oriented. We are a customer-service business, and we live and die by how well we do the little things. If you aren't willing to hold people accountable, you don't get excellence."

As we probed more deeply, we asked Paul to look closely at the costs and implications of his management style. Did he, for example, get angry and impatient with vendors and clients? Obviously not, he told us, because doing so would drive customers away. Why then, we asked, did he assume that his attitude wouldn't have a similarly negative effect on his employees? Why was he willing to treat them in a way that he would never consider treating clients?

Paul had arranged to come through our program with his wife, Olivia, and she pointed out to him that he also brought his anger and impatience home. His two children, now twelve and fourteen, were afraid of his outbursts and so, she acknowledged, was she. Olivia reminded him about an incident two years earlier in which his then ten-year-old son had accidentally left his coat on an airplane. Paul became enraged at him. The anger passed quickly but Olivia said that their son had never forgotten the incident. This information had a powerful impact on Paul. He was, he told us, deeply concerned about his long-term relation-

---

PAUL M.

Targeted Muscle: Patience
Performance Barrier: Impatient, overly critical
Desired Outcome: More positive relationships

RITUAL

"Kindness matters" mantra under pressure
Deep abdominal breath, relax muscles
Transform threat into opportunity
Sandwich technique for giving feedback
Take responsibility for behavior

ONE-TIME ACTION STEPS

▪ Shift workout from 5:00 A.M. to noon

---

ships with his children. His deepest desire, he realized, was to communicate support and encouragement to his two sons rather than frustration and criticism. Gradually he realized this was true for his employees as well.

We began by looking at what factors at the physical level might be influencing Paul's behavior. As the president of a health-club business, he kept himself in very good physical shape. At the same time, he had long believed that the only way to keep on top of a demanding business and to be a model of commitment was to keep pushing nonstop. To fit in his daily workout, he did it each morning at 5:00 a.m. when he awoke. As he looked more closely at his impatience and reactivity, he realized that they tended to grow throughout the day. We pointed out that the furious pace at which he worked might be a contributing factor. We encouraged him to try moving his workout to midday, not just to sustain his physical capacity but also as a means of getting mental and emotional recovery.

Paul was reluctant to take time off in the middle of the day, but he agreed to give it a try. Almost immediately, he discovered that the effect on his energy was significant. He was accustomed to finishing his early morning workouts feeling pumped up, but now the surge of positive energy came at a time of day when he was used to feeling edgier. He found himself facing the afternoons feeling renewed and more positive.

Despite this change, Paul's habits were deeply ingrained, especially under pressure. With that in mind, he began building a ritual around looking for opportunities throughout the day to strengthen the muscles of patience and kindness. For starters, any time that he found himself waiting in line at an airport, or stuck in traffic, or feeling frustrated with an employee or a family member, he determined to say to himself "Kindness matters." This simple mantra made him instantly aware of how he wanted to behave under pressure. In effect, it became an opportunity to do some emotional weight lifting.

In situations in which Paul's irritation continued to rise, he took a deep abdominal breath and relaxed the muscles in his shoulders and his face. Doing so helped to short-circuit his fight-or-flight response and reduce his level of arousal. Once he felt less reactive, he tried to think of a way of transforming his initial experience of frustration into an opportunity to make others feel better—most often with self-deprecating humor.

When Paul felt that it was important to deliver some sort of critical feedback at work, he began using something that we call the "sandwich" technique. He started interactions by making some sort of genuinely positive observation about the person's performance. Next, he framed his critical feedback not as a lecture but as a discussion, allowing for the possibility that his perception might not be entirely accurate. Finally, he ended with some sort of encouragement. This approach was a way not just to behave with more kindness and consideration, but also to increase the likelihood that what he said would be heard and absorbed without defensiveness.

The habits of a lifetime do not change overnight, but Paul did discover that whenever he was able to short-circuit his impatience or his instant judgments, he felt better about himself. This was so even in situations in which he didn't get the response he wanted. When he did lose his temper or speak too harshly to someone, he added one more element to his ritual: apologizing and taking responsibility as quickly as possible.

HOLDING OPPOSITES

The deepest expression of emotional capacity is the ability to experience a full range of feelings. Because it is so difficult for the mind to hold contradictory impulses, our tendency is to choose up sides, valuing certain emotional skills while neglecting and even disparaging others. We may overvalue toughness and undervalue tenderness, for example, or do just the reverse, when in fact both represent important emotional muscles in our lives. The same is true of many other opposites: self-control and spontaneity, honesty and compassion, generosity and thriftiness, openness and discretion, passion and detachment, patience and urgency, caution and boldness, confidence and humility.

Take a moment to consider how broad a range of emotional muscles you have in your own life. In all likelihood you will discover that you have considerably more strength on one side of the spectrum than on the other. Notice, too, the judgment that you bring to the relative merits of opposing qualities. No emotional capacity better serves depth and richness more than the willingness to value feelings that seem contradictory and not to choose up sides between them. To be fully engaged emotionally requires celebrating what the Stoic philosophers called *anacoluthia*—the mutual entailment of the virtues. By this notion, no virtue is a virtue by itself. Rather, all virtues are entailed. Honesty without compassion, for example, becomes cruelty.

We are, in effect, the sum of our complexities and contradictions. Practically, we must focus on building emotional capacity wherever it is that we are most out of balance. The ultimate goal is to move more freely and flexibly between our own opposites.

BEAR IN MIND

- In order to perform at our best, we must access pleasant and positive emotions: the experience of enjoyment, challenge, adventure and opportunity.
- The key muscles fueling positive emotional energy are self-confidence, self-control, interpersonal effectiveness and empathy.
- Negative emotions serve survival but they are very costly and energy inefficient in the context of performance.
- The ability to summon positive emotions during periods of intense stress lies at the heart of effective leadership.
- Access to the emotional muscles that serve

performance depends on creating a balance between exercising them regularly and intermittently seeking recovery.

- Any activity that is enjoyable, fulfilling and affirming serves as a source of emotional renewal and recovery.
- Emotional muscles such as patience, empathy and confidence can be strengthened in the same way that we strengthen a bicep or a tricep: pushing past our current limits followed by recovery.

CHAPTER 6

MENTAL ENERGY: APPROPRIATE FOCUS AND REALISTIC OPTIMISM

Just as physical energy is the fundamental fuel for emotional competencies, so it is the fuel for mental skills. Nothing so interferes with performance and engagement as the inability to concentrate on the task at hand. To perform at our best we must be able to sustain concentration, and to move flexibly between broad and narrow, as well as internal and external focus. We also need access to realistic optimism, a paradoxical notion that implies seeing the world as it is, but always working positively toward a desired outcome or solution. Anything that prompts appropriate focus and realistic optimism serves performance. The key supportive muscles that fuel optimal mental energy include mental preparation, visualization, positive self-talk, effective time management, and creativity.

Much as it is true physically and emotionally,

mental capacity is derived from a balance between expending and recovering energy. The capacity to stay appropriately focused and realistically optimistic depends on intermittently changing mental channels in order to rest and rejuvenate. When we lack the mental muscles we need to perform at our best—if we have too short an attention span, too pessimistic an outlook, or too rigid and narrow a perspective—we must build capacity by training systematically.

Physical, emotional and mental energy capacity all feed upon one another. At the physical level, the increased fatigue that results from too little sleep or poor fitness makes it more difficult to concentrate. At the emotional level feelings such as anxiety, frustration and anger interfere with focus and undermine optimism, especially in the face of high demand. We first learned these lessons in our work with athletes. One of the most vivid examples occurred in the late 1980s, when Jim received a call from middleweight boxing champion Ray "Boom Boom" Mancini, with whom he was then working.

"I'm really concerned," Mancini said. "I had a negative thought in the ring today."

"Just one negative thought?" Jim answered, a little incredulous.

"You don't understand, Doc," Mancini said. "A single negative thought is what gets you hit in the face."

In a less dramatic way, the same is true in other

148

performance venues. Psychologist Martin Seligman spent several years studying the relationship between positive thinking and sales success. Seligman developed an instrument called the Attributional Style Questionnaire (ASQ) to assess people's levels of optimism. This test was given to a large group of Metropolitan Life Insurance Company salesmen. When scores were matched to actual sales records, it turned out that agents who scored in the top half for optimism sold 37 percent more insurance over two years than those in the more pessimistic bottom half. More notable still, agents who scored in the top 10 percent for optimism sold 88 percent more than those ranked in the most pessimistic 10 percent. Agents who scored in the bottom 50 percent on the same test were twice as likely to leave their jobs as their more optimistic counterparts, while those in the bottom 25 percent were three times as likely to quit.

In our terms, it is the mental energy derived from positive thinking—what Seligman calls "optimistic explanatory style"—that drives the persistence of a successful salesman. Of course, it doesn't always serve us well to put a positive spin on events. Negative thoughts may help to direct our attention to important needs that aren't being met—whether for food, rest, emotional support or a danger that lurks on the horizon. To the extent that we listen to these signals and address them as quickly as possible, they serve a useful role in our lives. It is also important to be able to accurately assess situations and to avoid those in which the outcome is very likely to be negative or destructive. But this instinct is different than pessimism, which colors any perception and tends to be defensive rather than solution-based. When it comes to the everyday challenge of performance, the energy of negative thinking is almost invariably undermining and counterproductive. Realistic optimism better serves most of the challenges we face.

THINKING ASIDE

Perhaps nowhere do we so undervalue the importance of intermittent recovery as in the mental dimension of our lives. In most work environments, the message—both explicit and implicit— is that working longer and more continuously is the best route to high productivity. We aren't rewarded for taking regular breaks, or for building a workout into the middle of a day, or for any pattern of work other than keeping our heads down and grinding away for as long as we can.

The problem is that thinking uses up a great deal of energy. The brain represents just 2 percent of the body's weight, but requires almost 25 percent of its oxygen. The consequences of insufficient mental recovery range from increased mistakes of judgment and execution to lower creativity and a failure to take reasonable account of risks. The key to mental recovery is to give the conscious, thinking mind intermittent rest.

In his provocative book, *How to Think Like Leonardo da Vinci*, author Michael Gelb poses a wonderfully revealing question: "Where are you when you get your best ideas?" Gelb has asked this question to thousands of people over the years, and the most common answers he gets include "in the shower," "resting in bed," "walking in nature" and "listening to music." We ask our own clients a similar question and their answers have ranged from taking a jog to meditating to dreaming to sitting on the beach. "Almost no one," Gelb writes, "claims to get their best ideas at work."

Prolific and productive as Leonardo da Vinci was, Gelb points out, the artist took regular breaks from his work. Rather than sleeping extended hours at night, he relied on numerous catnaps during the day. While da Vinci was working on *The Last Supper*, he sometimes spent several hours in the middle of the day appearing to be lost in daydreams, in spite of entreaties from his employer, the prior of Santa Maria delle Grazie, to work more steadily. "The greatest geniuses," da Vinci told his patron, "sometimes accomplish more when they work less." In his *Treatise on Painting*, da Vinci wrote, "It is a very good plan every now and then to go away and have a little relaxation. . . . When you come back to the work your judgment will be surer, since to remain

151

constantly at work will cause you to lose the power of judgment."

CREATIVITY AND RECOVERY

Oscillation also permits different parts of the brain to be activated. The neurosurgeon Roger Sperry won a Nobel Prize in 1967 for research in which he established that the two hemispheres of the brain have fundamentally different ways of processing information. The left hemisphere is the seat of language and operates in a sequential, step-by-step, time-conscious way, arriving at conclusions based on logical deductions. Sperry's breakthrough was his discovery that the right hemisphere has unique and often underappreciated qualities of its own. It is more visually and spatially adept and has a greater capacity to see things all at once and to relate the parts to the whole. Because the right hemisphere is less linear and time-focused than the left, it is more inclined to solve problems by intuitive leap and sudden insight.

Sperry's work helps to explain why our best ideas often occur when we seem not to be consciously seeking solutions. Equally important, intermittent right-hemisphere dominance seems to provide a powerful form of recovery from the rational, analytic left-hemisphere mode that occupies most of our time at work.

The creative process itself is oscillatory.

Beginning with the German physiologist and physicist Hermann Helmholtz in the late nineteenth century, many thinkers have sought to define the sequential steps of the creative process. Five stages are now widely recognized: first insight, saturation, incubation, illumination and verification. In her books *Drawing on the Right Side of the Brain* and *Drawing on the Artist Within*, writer and art professor Betty Edwards has written brilliantly about the way that creativity involves cycling between the left and right hemisphere modes of thinking.

Two of the stages of creativity clearly depend more on logical, analytical left-hemisphere skills. In saturation, information is gathered in a methodical, step-by-step way from multiple sources. The final stage, verification, relies on analyzing, codifying and translating the creative breakthrough into rational, accessible language. The other three stages—first insight (the initial inspiration), incubation (mulling over the ideas), and illumination (the breakthrough)—are all associated with the right hemisphere. All three tend to occur when we are doing something that Edwards calls "thinking aside"—not actively seeking answers or results. "In each of these stages," she writes, "the creative work occurs largely at an unconscious level—and often after the left hemisphere's conscious, rational search for a solution has been exhausted." In short, the highest form of creativity depends on a rhythmic movement between engagement and disengagement, thinking and letting go, activity and rest. Both sides of the equation are necessary, but neither is sufficient by itself.

JAKE T.: MENTAL STALENESS

At age thirty-five, Jake T. ran a boutique marketing and advertising firm that he had founded. It was known for its novel, high-visibility campaigns for products aimed at younger Gen X and Gen Y consumers. After a long string of successes, the company had been hit by the combination of a declining economy and sudden competition from larger companies who had been slow to recognize a market opportunity. Energetic and ambitious by temperament, Jake responded by pushing himself and his people harder to break new creative ground. To his surprise and frustration, his efforts were proving counterproductive. Longer hours and more intense commitment weren't translating into more creative output. Jake came to us because he felt personally frustrated and exhausted and because the key members of his young team seemed to have lost their edge as well.

Given the firm's exceptional earlier success, it was clear that the problem wasn't a lack of talent or skill—either in Jake's case or more broadly in the organization. It struck us that he was effectively trying too hard—pushing himself relentlessly to be more creative and productive, and

JAKE T.

Targeted Muscle: Creativity
Performance Barrier: Mental staleness
Desired Outcome: Increased energy, higher
  creativity

RITUAL

Mon, Wed, Fri 5:30–7:30 A.M.: Painting
Mon–Friday 10:30–10:45 A.M.: Yoga
Mon–Friday 1:00–1:30 P.M.: Get outside for
  lunch
Mon–Friday 4:00–4:30 P.M.: Yoga

ONE-TIME ACTION STEPS

■ Set up yoga/meditation room in office
■ Buy Ping-Pong table

doing the same to his staff. We suggested to Jake
that he was spending too much mental energy
without sufficient recovery, and that the answer
might be to build in more down time to think in
different ways, and to allow ideas to percolate.
What activities outside work, we asked, did he
especially enjoy? Jake came up with several,
although he admitted that he loved his work above
all, and that he had spent very little time on
anything else during the past several years.

Up through college, Jake had aspirations to be
a painter, only to give it up completely when he

concluded that he didn't have the goods to make a living at it. Even so, he remembered painting as a source of immense pleasure, something that he found both challenging and deeply absorbing. With our encouragement, Jake decided to buy new supplies and take up painting again. He was too tired to paint when he got home at night, but he loved the idea of waking up early and spending an hour or two in front of the easel in the mornings. It cleared his mind of the pressures at work and shifted him into the right-hemisphere mode that facilitates creativity. On several occasions, ideas for marketing campaigns occurred to him while he was painting. He also found that he was looser and more imaginative during the first several morning hours at work.

The second form of recovery that Jake embraced was yoga. A basketball player during high school and college, he retained his passion for the game through his twenties, but gave it up in his thirties partly in response to the demands of work and partly because he got tired of dealing with jammed fingers, twisted ankles and sprained knees. Jake had done a good deal of yoga during college—his basketball coach used it as a stretching exercise— and he was reintroduced to the practice during his training with us. Like many of our clients, he found it relaxing mentally and emotionally, and energizing physically. He began building two "yoga" breaks into his workday—ten to fifteen minutes when he closed his office door and did a half dozen postures. He found them so rejuvenating, especially in the afternoons, that it occurred to him that others in the firm might have the same experience.

Jake decided to set aside a room at the office just for yoga and meditation, and he even offered to teach a class once a week. Even on the days that he was traveling, he built in time for yoga, in the early morning and before dinner and at the end of his workday. He also bought a Ping-Pong table for the office and he encouraged people to get out for lunch and leave their work behind. Following up on one of our principles, he told his staff that he was less interested in how much time they devoted to their jobs than in the quality of energy they brought to their tasks.

Jake worried at first that he was taking a risk in encouraging his employees to build intermittent breaks into their days. Some of them might take advantage of his new policy simply to slack off. But he also reasoned that selectively slacking off might actually fuel their creativity. In his own case, taking time for painting before work and building yoga into his days significantly changed both the quality and the quantity of his energy and his productivity. It not only increased his capacity for focus when he was working, but it seemed to open access to a whole new level of creativity.

Over the next several months, the atmosphere in the company changed noticeably, Jake told us. It became looser, more playful and more spirited—not unlike its earliest days when there were a half dozen employees seeking to build a new business rather than seventy trying to sustain one. Jake himself felt rejuvenated and the imaginativeness of the company's marketing campaigns soared. Their work reacquired a buzz in the industry. It was, Jake believed, as if the whole company had awakened from a slumber.

THE PLASTICITY OF THE BRAIN

Increasing evidence confirms that the brain itself operates like a muscle—atrophying from disuse and increasing in capacity with active use, even late in life. At Baylor College of Medicine, a research team spent four years studying nearly one hundred physically healthy people over the age of sixty-four. One third of them still had jobs. One third had retired but remained active physically and mentally. The final third had retired and were essentially inactive. After four years, the third group scored significantly lower than the first two, not just on IQ tests but also on those measuring blood flow to their brains. As neurologist Richard Restak puts it: "No matter how old you may be at this moment, it's never too late to change your brain for the better. That's because the brain is different from every other organ in our body. While the liver and the lungs and the kidneys wear out after a certain number of years, the brain gets sharper the more it's used. Indeed it improves with use."

Because the mind and body are so inextricably connected, even moderate physical exercise can increase cognitive capacity. It does so most simply by driving more blood and oxygen to the brain. Exercise is also believed to stimulate more production of a chemical—brain-derived neurotrophic factor—which helps repair brain cells and prevent further damage. A research team at the University of Illinois set out to test the cognitive functioning of 124 women ages sixty to seventy-five who never or rarely exercised. The women were put on a three-day-a-week program that included either a brisk one-hour walk or an hour of gentle yoga-style stretching. In effect the exercisers were asked to push past their comfort zones physically, while the stretchers were not. After just six months, the walkers demonstrated 25 percent higher scores than the stretchers on a series of key cognitive tests. In a similar experiment, a Japanese neuroscientist put a group of young people on a jogging program of thirty minutes, two to three times a week. When he tested them at the end of twelve weeks on a series of memory skills, their scores significantly increased, and so did the speed with which they completed the tests. Of equal note, their gains disappeared almost immediately when they stopped jogging.

Epidemiologist David Snowden's nuns study suggests that ongoing intellectual activity wards off deterioration. No single factor better predicted the risk of eventual Alzheimer's, for example, than the density of ideas and the grammatical complexity of the biographical essays that nuns in the study wrote about themselves in their twenties. More compelling still, Snowden found that nuns who taught for most of their lives showed significantly less mental decline than those who had devoted themselves to less intellectually challenging forms of service.

Much as it is true physically and emotionally, the balance of stress and recovery appears to be a critical factor in maximizing cognitive capacity. Exposing one's self to short-term stress, for example, can stimulate a burst of adrenaline that actually improves memory. When the demand is more linear and chronic—and stress hormones continue to circulate in the brain—the hippocampus can actually shrink. Much like the body, the brain needs time to recover from exertion. After we have learned new information or had new experiences, it takes time for the brain to consolidate and encode what it has learned. In the absence of downtime, or recovery, this learning cannot take place as efficiently.

Loss of memory is the most common complaint that people over the age of forty bring to neurologists. Far more often than not, the explanation is not disease, but rather the failure to actively keep the mind engaged, and the resulting atrophy of the "muscles" of memory. Much as is the case physically, disuse feeds on itself. When we are young and our brains are highly plastic, learning

160

even complex skills such as language is relatively easy. As we get older, and exercise these muscles less, the challenge of learning a new language or a new skill tends to be more difficult and frustrating. To avoid discomfort (and in some cases humiliation) our inclination is to give up. The result is that the avoidable deterioration of our capacity continues.

"Every time you learn something new it builds new connections to the brain cells," says Margery Silver, assistant professor of psychology at Harvard Medical School and associate director of the New England Centenarian study, "That way if you do have a few changes—a few plaques and tangles associated with Alzheimer's and a few brain cells become damaged, you still have a reserve because of all these additional connections you built up." Put another way, continuing to challenge the brain protects us from decline as we age. Just as learning a new sport forces us to build new muscles and to use our bodies in different ways, so learning new computer skills, or taking a new course, or even learning a few new words of vocabulary each day pushes us to develop the mental muscles that serve performance.

ALICE P.: PESSIMISM, NEGATIVITY

A partner in a middle-size law firm, Alice had an almost unerring eye for what might go wrong in any situation. She could pick up the one small grammatical error in an otherwise flawless thirty-page brief. She could spot a small shortcoming in the most desirable candidate for a job. She could find good reasons not to take on a new client or to expand the size of the firm or even to hold a Christmas party. This capacity made her a one-woman insurance policy against disaster. It also made her the purveyor of a relentlessly critical and pessimistic energy—the sort of person no one wanted to spend much time around. Worse, her negativity was so predictable that over time her colleagues began to discount her point of view.

Alice continued to believe that she was the only person in her company willing to look squarely at the truth. It never occurred to her in some cases her approach might be only one part of the truth or that by focusing so narrowly on specific issues, she might be losing sight of the larger picture. Nor did she take into account the impact that her negative energy had on her own effectiveness or on others.

Alice's first breakthrough in working with us was the recognition that she was stuck in one limited way of looking at the world—namely negatively. It robbed her of much satisfaction or joy, not just at work but also in her personal life. If she went on a vacation with her husband and two teenage sons, she admitted, she was the one who found something wrong with the hotel room or the food or the weather. If one of her sons came home with an A on a test, she immediately focused on a

ALICE P.

Targeted Muscle: Realistic optimism
Performance Barrier: Pessimism, negative
  thinking
Desired Outcome: Positive, solution-based
  thinking

RITUAL

7:00 A.M.: Sit down and write perceived
  threats in a journal and then recast them
  as opportunities
Consider worst-case scenarios and assess
  whether consequences are acceptable
Focus on aspects of life worthy of appreciation

subject in which he wasn't doing as well. If her other son scored a touchdown for his high school football team but sustained a small ankle injury, she focused on the dangers of football rather than her son's success.

Over time, Alice built a series of routines to mobilize more positive solution-based thinking. None so affected the pattern of her thinking as the ritual that she instituted in the mornings when she woke up. To start each day, she wrote down in a journal everything that she felt was going wrong in her life, or might go wrong. These might range from "The brief I'm writing isn't going well" to "I said the wrong thing to a client today and

163

jeopardized our relationship" to "The associate on this case just can't cut it, and he's wasting my time."

Next, Alice tried to step back from the perceived crisis and recast it not as a catastrophe and a threat but as a challenge and an opportunity. In effect, this became a weight-training session for realistic optimism. If it was the brief she was worrying about, she might focus on the fact that she had written dozens of them before and that struggling was a necessary part of the process of getting it right. If she was worried about a client, she might remind herself that she already had a long relationship in place and that the misstep created an opportunity to learn and to be more effective in the future. If it was the work of an associate she felt upset about, she might focus on his strengths and take pleasure in the chance to serve as a mentor and pass along her considerable knowledge.

In order to feel more secure, Alice decided it was critical to create an escape hatch for situations that she believed, even after reflection, merited concern and skepticism. In those instances, she asked herself the question, "What is the worst-case scenario here? If everything that could go wrong did go wrong, could I live with the consequences?" In nearly every case, she discovered that she could, which she found reassuring. This lowered her level of urgency and allowed her to make her suggestions in less apocalyptic terms.

Alice ended her early morning ritual by focusing on those aspects of her life for which she felt thankful and appreciative. No part of Alice's ritual was more satisfying than this one. It helped her to appreciate how extraordinarily fortunate she was in nearly every aspect of her life—the fact that she had her health, reasonable financial security, a husband and two sons she loved as well as a job that she still found challenging.

On most mornings, this exercise prompted a welcome shift in Alice's energy. Physically, she became more relaxed. Emotionally, she felt more hopeful. Mentally, she became less distracted, more flexible and better able to concentrate. These experiences fed on one another, prompting a greater sense of engagement in her work. In time, this process became an almost automatic response to any persistent negative thought. Only when the pressures were unusually high did it become necessary for Alice to take herself more formally through this morning exercise.

In effect, Alice redirected the energy she had been devoting to spotting what was wrong with the world and began applying it instead to looking for what was right. Retaining the option to raise a red flag at times kept her from feeling like a Polyanna. Under pressure, her highly critical eye and her pessimism sometimes resurfaced, but rarely for long. For the first time in her adult life, she felt fueled by possibility rather than by fear.

SARA D.:
POOR TIME MANAGEMENT,
LOW ATTENTION SPAN

Sara D. worked as a hospital administrator and fought what she felt was a losing battle for control over her life. At thirty-five, she was single and lived alone. The fact that she didn't have family responsibilities gave her the freedom to work as many hours as she chose. It also made it very hard for her to leave her office at the end of the day. A problem solver by instinct, she was the one to whom everyone seemed to turn in a crisis. The result was that her time never felt like her own. Mail, memos and unfinished projects piled high on her desk. Sara told us that she admired both efficiency and creativity, and that because she had so little of the former, she seemed to find no time for the latter.

Time management, we tell our clients, is not an end in itself. Rather it serves the higher goal of effective energy management. Because we have a limited number of hours in a day, we must not only make intelligent choices about how to use them but must also insure that we have the energy available to invest in our highest priorities. Too often, we devote our time to activities that don't advance our mission, depleting our energy reserves in the process. Stephen Covey captures this deftly in *The 7 Habits of Highly Effective People* when he describes how often the urgent in our lives—what seems most demanding in the moment—crowds out the important—priorities that are ultimately more consequential, but don't necessarily require immediate attention. The same is true of many corporate cultures, where a constant sense of emergency makes it difficult for anyone to step back and make more thoughtful choices.

Urgency was precisely Sara's issue. Fiercely action oriented, she was forever reacting to the demands of others. Phone calls, emails, and people arriving at her door with pressing concerns consumed her energy all day long. Creative brainstorming, reflection and attending to longer-range planning and writing projects all tended to get pushed aside. Partly the issue was her attention span. Like many of our clients, Sara found it difficult to concentrate on any one subject for long. While she took a certain pride in her multitasking ability—answering email while she talked on the phone, for example—the result was that she rarely gave all of her attention to anything. Her staff had learned that if an issue couldn't be summarized in a few bullet points, Sara wasn't likely to absorb it. Unfortunately, not every issue lends itself to simple resolution. This is especially true when it comes to people's personal issues, rather than specific tasks. Although she was nurturing by nature, Sara was increasingly perceived as rushed and unavailable.

The first ritual that Sara decided to launch was to spend twenty to thirty minutes when she awoke

SARA D.

Targeted Muscle: Time management
Performance Barrier: Disorganized, distracted
Desired Outcome: Efficiency, appropriate focus

RITUAL

6:00–6:30 A.M.: Reflection, journaling, to do list

7:30–8:00 A.M.: Mental preparation (commute)

8:00–9:00 A.M.: Project time

10:30 A.M., 3:30 P.M.: Cafeteria breaks

7:00 P.M. Mon, Wed, Th: Aerobics class

ONE-TIME ACTION STEPS

■ Buy journal, personal organizer

■ Clean up desk, create efficient filing system

■ Tell staff about "Do Not Disturb" times

in the mornings shifting her attention from her usual external focus to an internal one. She wrote in a journal about issues both at work and in her personal life. Writing helped her to feel that she wasn't simply a work machine, and it also gave her a chance to reflect on her relationships, on and off the job. Next, Sara took ten to fifteen minutes to compose a to-do list for the day ahead in the personal organizer that we persuaded her to purchase. Sara had always resisted the idea of lists, but she acknowledged that the demands in her life had exceeded her capacity to keep track of all of them. Finally, during her thirty-minute commute to work, Sara built a mental preparation ritual—thinking through the day ahead, and visualizing how she wanted to handle the specific challenges that she faced.

It took Sara more than a month to get these initial rituals in place, in part because she resisted at first being captive to such a fixed schedule. What she discovered over time was that the morning rituals actually gave her a greater sense of calmness and focus, which made her feel freer and less under siege. Once her morning rituals became relatively automatic, she committed to changing the way that she managed her priorities when she got to work. Her usual practice was to move immediately into reactive mode—reading the previous night's accumulated email or answering voice mail or responding to someone at her door. Instead, she decided to devote the first sixty minutes to whatever project she had deemed most important. Sara chose 8:00 to 9:00 a.m. for this work, both because it was when she felt freshest and because the demands on her time grew as the day wore on. She told her secretary that she did not want to be interrupted during these sixty minutes except in the case of an emergency.

Sara mostly used this early morning time for writing projects, which had previously consumed her weekends. Launching her days by being productive on a project of her own choosing gave her a sense of accomplishment and an energy boost for the rest of the day. Sara also committed to taking an aerobics class at 7:00 p.m. three nights a week, which forced her to leave work, served as a source of mental and emotional recovery after demanding days, and created an effective transition between work and home.

Finally, Sara became almost religious about building two breaks into her day as a means of insuring intermittent recovery. The hospital cafeteria was on another floor, and she made it her business to go there at 10:30 a.m. and then again at 3:30 p.m. for at least five to ten minutes. Events didn't always make it possible to take breaks at exactly these times, so Sara simply took them as close to the designated times as she possibly could. Modest as the breaks were, they provided a way to escape the maelstrom for a few moments, to eat a piece of fruit or drink a cup of tea, and to regroup.

Failing to respond instantly to people's requests was very difficult for Sara at first. By the second month, however, the increased freedom, clarity and productivity she felt far outweighed her guilt. Because she was more focused and productive, she also found that she was more comfortable taking time with people, both about strategic issues at work, and about their personal concerns—especially at the end of the workday. To her surprise, the new structure in her life gave her a sense of freedom and relaxed energy.

BEAR IN MIND

- Mental capacity is what we use to organize our lives and focus our attention.
- The mental energy that best serves full engagement is realistic optimism—seeing the world as it is, but always working positively towards a desired outcome or solution.
- The key supportive mental muscles include mental preparation, visualization, positive self-talk, effective time management and creativity.
- Changing channels mentally permits different parts of the brain to be activated and facilitates creativity.
- Physical exercise stimulates cognitive capacity.
- Maximum mental capacity is derived from a balance between expending and recovering mental energy.
- When we lack the mental muscles we need to perform at our best, we must systematically build capacity by pushing past our comfort zone and then recovering.
- Continuing to challenge the brain serves as a protection against age-related mental decline.

CHAPTER 7

SPIRITUAL ENERGY:
HE WHO HAS A WHY TO LIVE

The quantity of energy we have to spend at any given moment is a reflection of our physical capacity. Our motivation to spend what we have is largely a spiritual issue. Fundamentally, spiritual energy is a unique force for action in all dimensions of our lives. It is the most powerful source of our motivation, perseverance and direction. We define "spiritual" not in the religious sense, but rather in more simple and elemental terms: the connection to a deeply held set of values and to a purpose beyond our self-interest. At the practical level, anything that ignites the human spirit serves to drive full engagement and to maximize performance in whatever mission we are on. The key muscle that fuels spiritual energy is character—the courage and conviction to live by our values, even when doing so requires personal sacrifice and hardship. Supportive spiritual muscles include passion, commitment, integrity and honesty.

Spiritual energy is sustained by balancing a commitment to others with adequate self-care. Put another way, the capacity to live by our deepest values depends on regularly renewing our spirit—seeking ways to rest and rejuvenate and to reconnect with the values that we find most inspiring and meaningful. When we lack sufficient spiritual energy, we must find systematic ways to go deeper—to challenge our complacency and expediency. In Roger B.'s case, the disconnection from a compelling sense of purpose had robbed him of passion and of any clear sense of direction. He operated instead in survival mode, doing what was necessary to fill immediate needs and to get by day-to-day. Often, he felt like a victim. Roger didn't think much about the long-term consequences of his choices largely because he didn't have a vision of what he wanted from life or where he was headed. The result was that all of his energy systems were compromised.

It is often around tragedy that people discover the importance of spiritual energy. When the actor Christopher Reeve became a quadriplegic following a horseback-riding accident in 1995, it would hardly have been surprising if he had felt overcome by despair. Very briefly, he said later, he contemplated suicide. But within a short time, Reeve managed to tap into a fierce source of spiritual energy—the desire to continue to be there for his family, to help find a cure for his condition and to continue to make a contribution in the world—not least by serving as an inspiration for others in his situation. This fierce sense of purpose helped Reeve to mobilize hope and optimism and to move forward with focus and clarity, even with a severely compromised source of physical energy and a dramatically increased vulnerability to fear, frustration and despair. Spiritual energy effectively saved his life.

The employees of the bond trading company Cantor Fitzgerald collectively drew upon a deep reservoir of spiritual energy in the face of a very different tragedy. The company's headquarters was on four of the top floors of One World Trade Center, and more than two-thirds of the one thousand employees in Cantor's New York offices died on September 11, 2001. The company's computer systems and massive amounts of data were also destroyed, and it was unclear whether Cantor itself could survive. The remaining employees were understandably shocked, grief-stricken and in many cases traumatized. In energy terms, the physical, emotional and mental drain on their energy capacity was enormous.

What allowed Cantor's employees to move forward, it turned out, was tapping into a compelling sense of purpose. Efforts to save the firm certainly served their own financial needs, but their cause became much bigger than that. Within days, Howard Lutnick, Cantor's chairman, announced that 25 percent of any profits the firm earned during the subsequent five years would go to the families of employees who had lost their lives. This decision mobilized the remaining employees to fight for a purpose beyond themselves. The survivors became "a band of brothers," as one of them put it, drawn together by the shared tragedy and the challenge ahead.

The result was a fierce level of dedication. Employees began to work twelve- to sixteen-hour days. According to Heidi Olson, an employee who had left the firm but felt compelled to return after September 11: "Everything we took for granted was gone. So I just did whatever had to be done. It is like being a mom—in that spiritual sense of doing whatever is needed for the good of the family." Along the way, Cantor Fitzgerald employees discovered previously untapped emotional resources—patience, compassion, the ability to uncomplainingly endure difficult makeshift working conditions—that helped them get through the trauma. Their commitment to a higher mission helped them to focus and persevere for long hours, even as they operated on limited sleep. If there was a risk in the long term, it was that the failure to adequately replenish their physical, mental and emotional energy reserves might eventually prompt burnout and breakdown. In any case, it is hard to imagine a more vivid example of the profound source of spiritual energy that can be tapped—even in the worst adversity—

by a shared vision and a commitment to a mission larger than one's self.

To understand the significance of purpose on a more everyday level, consider the case of Ann F., a high-level executive at a large cosmetics company. For much of her adult life, Ann had tried unsuccessfully to quit smoking, blaming her failure on a lack of self-discipline. Smoking took a quiet but undeniable toll on her health and her productivity at work—decreased endurance from shortness of breath, more sick days than her colleagues, and nicotine cravings that distracted her during long meetings. She was obviously aware that smoking put her at considerably higher risk of an early death. On the other hand, smoking provided a strong source of sensory pleasure, and it was a way to allay her anxiety and to manage social stress. Above all, the physical addiction had an overwhelming hold over her.

On the day that Ann learned she was pregnant for the first time, she decided to quit smoking right then and there. Until the day that her child was born, she never picked up another cigarette. She resumed smoking before she had left the hospital. A year later, Ann became pregnant for a second time, and once again she stopped smoking for the subsequent nine months. As she had the first time, she was easily able to overcome her intermittent cravings, but true to her first experience, she resumed smoking right after her second child was born. "I don't understand it," she told us plaintively.

The explanation was actually very simple. When Ann was able to connect the impact of smoking to a deeper purpose—the health of her unborn child—she gained access to a wellspring of focused purpose. Quitting was easy. Once her child was born and she no longer had such a clear sense of purpose, the lure of smoking became compelling again. Understanding cognitively that it was unhealthy to smoke, feeling guilty about it on an emotional level, and even experiencing its negative effects physically were all insufficient motivations to change her behavior.

To quit smoking, Ann needed the unique motivation that comes from connecting to a spiritual source of energy. We helped her to reconnect to that energy in three ways. The first was simply to point out that secondhand smoke is itself insidious, and that if she continued smoking she would be exposing her children to a health hazard, as well as sending a signal to them that smoking is acceptable. We also pushed Ann to face the reality that continuing to smoke increased dramatically the odds that her children would grow up without a mother. Because family and concern for others were among her key values, they became a source of motivation to quit smoking. Finally, we helped Ann to acknowledge that smoking was a primary cause of her poor health and her low energy, both of which took a serious toll on her performance at work and ultimately on her capacity to be engaged at home.

More than at any other level, spiritual energy expenditure and renewal are deeply intertwined and tend to occur simultaneously. Nearly all contemplative traditions talk about spiritual "work" and spiritual "practice." These activities may be aimed at being of service to others or deepening our compassion or helping us to experience our interconnectedness. Spiritual renewal, on the other hand, comes from feeling inspired by and reconnected to our sense of purpose and our deepest values.

Some activities generate considerable spiritual renewal without demanding significant energy expenditure. These include walking in nature, reading an inspirational book, listening to music, or hearing a great speaker. Spiritual practices, by contrast, can be renewing and demanding at the same time. Meditation, for example, requires mobilizing highly focused attention to quiet the mind, but may also prompt a rejuvenating experience of expansive openness, connectedness and even joy. Like yoga, meditation is a practice that can cut across all dimensions, building spiritual capacity while also providing mental and emotional recovery.

Prayer, too, requires the effort of concentration and contemplation, but can also serve as a source of emotional and spiritual comfort. Reflecting regularly on our deepest values and holding ourselves accountable to them is both difficult and taxing, but it may also be inspiring and energizing. At a more basic level, devoting time and energy to our children can be both a spiritual "practice"—sacrificing our own pressing needs for theirs—and also a rich source of renewal, emotionally and spiritually. The same is true of all service to others, which involves considerable effort and even inconvenience, but may also provide a profound source of meaning and deep satisfaction.

GARY A.: APATHY, DISAFFECTION

At forty-seven, Gary A. was a top executive at a large financial services firm. After twenty years with the company, he felt increasingly disengaged. He had begun to question why exactly he was doing his job, and whether it was really worth it. He was generously compensated, but the more we talked with him, the more it became clear that he hungered to do more than just increase his net worth and climb the executive ladder in his company. He felt a parallel hunger in his personal life. He and his wife had divorced ten years earlier, and while they shared custody of their two daughters, his travel schedule and long hours had limited his time with them. Both daughters were now in their twenties, living in different cities, and his regrets ran deep, especially about the lost opportunities to connect with them through their shared love of sports. While Gary had been an excellent athlete himself, and both girls had played soccer and basketball all through high school, he had rarely made it to any of their games.

GARY A.

Targeted Muscle: Passion
Performance Barrier: Disaffection, detachment
Desired Outcome: Commitment, full
engagement

RITUAL

M, W, F 5:30–7:00 P.M., Saturday mornings:
Coach basketball
Tuesday 7:00 A.M.: Breakfast with direct
report
Thursday 6:00 P.M.: Drinks with direct
report

When we asked Gary what might give him a greater sense of meaning and purpose in his life, he couldn't come up with an answer at work. Once we opened the possibility to the rest of his life, he answered without missing a beat: "Coaching kids." It was too late with his own kids, he said, but coaching struck him as a way that he could make a contribution and feel fulfilled. It happened that Gary lived near a group foster home for orphans and children whose parents had been deemed unfit to care for them. Gary had passed the home on his way to work for years and barely given it a second thought. Now he decided to try volunteering his services. As it happened, the administration was looking for someone to coach its boy's basketball team. The job required a commitment of three nights a week, along with games on most Saturdays, but Gary was determined to do it.

His obvious skill as a player won him instant respect, but it was his nurturing style that eventually won the hearts of the kids on the team. Gary was sixteen when his own father died, and his high school basketball coach's steadfast encouragement and support, even when Gary's play fell off dramatically, had been deeply meaningful to him. The kids he was now coaching had even more harrowing stories to tell—of being abandoned, beaten, abused—and Gary saw a way to use basketball to build both their self-confidence and their connections with each other.

It didn't happen quickly. Gary spent the first several weeks of practice breaking up fights and trying with limited success to get the kids to keep their attention on practice. The team lost its first three games, and Gary had to throw one of the most talented players off the team after he physically assaulted a teammate. But Gary's patience and persistence eventually bore fruit. The team began to win its share of games, but even more than that, they began to genuinely work together as a team. For Gary, the rewards were immense. He loved coaching and he loved the kids. The exhilaration he felt spilled over into the rest of his life. For the first time in years, he felt alive and connected.

Three months after he first visited us—a month into his coaching—it dawned on Gary that there was an obvious parallel opportunity at work: serving as a mentor to the younger people who worked for him. The company had never rewarded nor given much priority to this role—or to leadership generally—but to Gary the analogies to coaching suddenly seemed obvious. Here was another chance to make a real difference. He launched a ritual around spending time away from work with the young traders in his department. His interest was not so much in improving their technical skills as it was in helping them to manage their careers and sort out their priorities, both at work and in the rest of their lives.

This proved especially significant as the stock market began to melt down. Gary's steadiness in the face of the downturn and his refusal to panic proved to be invaluable to many of his traders. He spent many breakfasts and lunches simply listening to them. In addition to offering counsel on how to navigate a difficult environment—and serving as a role model—he helped them to see that their self-worth didn't have to rise and fall with the market. Several of them even followed his lead and volunteered at different social service organizations. One actually became his assistant coach.

Demanding as it was to take time for his traders amid the pressures of a difficult market, Gary found it both rewarding and energizing. For the first time in two years, he started to look forward to coming to work, and to feel a sense of mission. The rewards that he derived from his mentoring—both at work and with his basketball team—gave him back far more energy than he expended.

"WHAT LIFE EXPECTS FROM US"

Expanding spiritual capacity requires subordinating our own needs to something beyond our self-interest. Because we often perceive our own needs as urgent, shifting attention away from them can prompt very primitive survival fears. If I truly focus my attention on others, we worry, who is going to look out for me? It is a mark of courage to set aside self-interest in order to be of service to others or to a cause. The irony is that self-absorption ultimately drains energy and impedes performance. The more preoccupied we are with our own fears and concerns, the less energy we have available to take positive action.

Subordinating our self-interest to something beyond ourselves may feel threatening at first, but as Gary discovered, it can also be immensely rewarding—a means by which to experience a deeper sense of meaning and greater self-worth. The commitment to live according to our deepest values not only creates a more stable center in our lives but also helps us to better navigate the challenges we face along the way.

Viktor Frankl has written movingly about the

power of spiritual capacity to transform even the most horrifying circumstances. Frankl was the psychologist who survived the Nazi concentration camps and went on to write the classic *Man's Search for Meaning*. In it he quotes Nietzsche's famous words, "He who has a why to live for can bear with almost any how." Frankl goes on to describe the way this insight helped to save his own life, even as others were dying around him:

Woe to him who saw no more sense in his life, no aim, no purpose, and therefore no point in carrying on. He was soon lost. What was needed was a fundamental change in our attitude toward life. We had to learn ourselves and, furthermore, we had to teach the despairing men, that it did not really matter what we expected from life, but rather what life expected from us. We needed to stop asking about the meaning of life, and instead to think of ourselves as those who were being questioned by life—hourly and daily. Our answer must consist not in talk and meditation, but in right action and in right conduct. Life ultimately means taking the responsibility to find the right answers to its problems and to fulfill the tasks which it constantly sets for each individual.

As Frankl saw it, we must make our own meaning—actively build spiritual capacity. Doing so necessarily involves discomfort. "Mental health is based on a certain degree of tension," he wrote, "the tension between what one has already achieved and what one still ought to accomplish, or the gap between what one is and what one should become. . . . What man actually needs is not a tensionless state, but rather the striving and struggling for a worthwhile goal, a freely chosen task."

Lance Armstrong offers a particularly inspiring example. In the early 1990s, Armstrong was a top American cyclist and by his own description, highly self-absorbed. In 1996, at the age of twenty-five, he was diagnosed with a virulent form of testicular cancer. In a short time, it spread to his lungs, and then to his brain. His odds of survival were put at less than 3 percent. Somehow Armstrong survived and, equally miraculously, he returned to cycling. In 1999, three years after his original cancer diagnosis, he won the Tour de France, the most challenging bicycle race in the world—and he went on to win it the next three years as well. As Armstrong saw it, surviving cancer was a far greater and more significant achievement—in large part because it pushed him beyond his own narrow ambitions:

The truth is that if you asked me to choose between winning the Tour de France and cancer, I would choose cancer. Odd as it sounds, I would rather have the title of cancer survivor than winner of the tour, because of what it has done for me as a human being, a man, a husband, a son and a father. . . . The one thing the illness has convinced me of beyond all doubt—more than any experience I've had as an athlete—is that we are much better than we know. We have unrealized capacities that sometimes only emerge in crisis. So if there is a purpose to the suffering that is cancer, I think it must be this: it's meant to improve us.

VALUING OTHERS

Barry F. was the CEO of a large information services company, and he thought of himself as a benevolent boss who treated his employees well. Nonetheless, one of the most consistent pieces of feedback he got from his direct reports was that he persistently kept them waiting and seemed not to value their time. This was a criticism, he acknowledged, that he had received for many years, and he couldn't deny its truth. Unfortunately, he told us, there was nothing he could do about it. Barry's daily schedule as CEO was packed. He never purposely kept anyone waiting, but calls and other demands piled up and he didn't express much hope of changing his behavior.

That perception changed dramatically during our work on identifying the values that Barry held most dear. He was unequivocal in identifying the number one value in his life: respect for others. Both of his parents had modeled this behavior and he spoke about it with great conviction.

"How then," we asked, "does respect for others square with keeping people waiting?"

There was a long silence. "It doesn't," he said finally.

When it came time to create Barry's action plan, respecting people's time became one of his primary commitments. When we spoke to Barry several months later, he told us that keeping on schedule had been difficult at first. He worried that he would antagonize the chairman of his company, members of his own board and key clients if he tried to end meetings with them at a specific time. What made it possible was reconnecting to the value he placed on respect for others. "The first thing I did was get more focused about covering my agenda in the time allotted," he explained. "In cases where time begins to run out and we still aren't finished, I now simply stop and explain that I am very sorry, but that I have made it a policy not to keep people waiting and that we'll have to schedule more time later. What I found is that it seems to make even the people I am meeting with feel more respected. It also makes them much more efficient about getting through their agendas." Simply acknowledging how important he felt it was to respect others gave Barry the determination to make a change that had eluded him for years.

JEREMY G.: INDECISIVE, CONFLICT-AVOIDANT

At thirty-seven, Jeremy G. worked as the business manager for the Internet division of a large consumer company committed to selling more of its products through the Web. Brilliant at creating deal structures and working creatively with numbers, Jeremy was charged with helping the company build a Web presence quickly while minimizing the company's financial exposure. By his own view and that of his colleagues, his primary performance barrier was his difficulty in taking a strong stand and his discomfort with conflict.

Jeremy told us that he simply felt more comfortable when people got along, and that he preferred not to make waves. He resisted the suggestion that he told people what he thought they wanted to hear, but he acknowledged that it was very important to him to be well liked. He was so attuned to how others were feeling—about him and about whatever issue was on the table—that he often found it hard to identify what he really felt himself. On the one hand, this made him an empathic listener and an easy person to be around. On the other hand, it made him passive and indecisive, which had long since prompted his colleagues to stop looking to him for insight. Rather than being a significant voice in strategy discussions, he served largely as the person who ran the numbers.

It never occurred to Jeremy that the obstacle he

JEREMY G.

Targeted Muscle: Resolve

Performance Barrier: Indecisive, conflict-
  avoidant

Desired Outcome: Clarity, conviction

RITUAL

Mentally prepare for meetings by visualizing
  self giving feedback

Set aside time for research prior to meetings

Ask: "What do I really believe?" "Is there
  anyone I'm trying to please with this
  answer?"

faced was primarily spiritual and that what he
lacked was access to the focused energy that comes
from connecting to one's deepest values. His challenge, we suggested, was to shift his orientation
from placating his bosses and worrying so much
about what they thought about him to trusting
his own voice and taking clear stands based on
their merits. That didn't mean he had to be
confrontational or antagonizing. He could still
treat others with respect while holding his own
ground.

When it came to creating an appropriate ritual,
we suggested that Jeremy begin by building mental
preparation time into every morning. Doing so
would give him a chance to rehearse his remarks

before prospective meetings, and to visualize his suggestions being accepted and valued. From our work with athletes we learned that visualizing a performance challenge in advance is a very effective way to allay anxiety and to perform without awkwardness or self-consciousness. Jeremy also decided to set aside time before meetings to research the subject to be discussed, in order to be fully informed even about issues outside his expertise.

The third dimension of Jeremy's ritual was designed for the meetings themselves. As issues arose, he asked himself a simple question "What do I really believe here?" and then tried to listen for his instinctive response. Doing so, he found, helped him avoid being distracted by other points of view. If he found himself agreeing with a point of view too readily, he asked himself a second question: "Who am I trying to please here?" It proved to be a highly effective way for Jeremy to ensure that he was speaking from a place of conviction.

LINDA P.: LACK OF FOLLOW-THROUGH, UNRELIABILITY

Linda P. was an executive in charge of buyers for a large department store chain. She had a dozen people reporting directly to her, and two hundred people in her division. Linda came to see us largely because she felt overwhelmed by her job and unable to create any sense of balance in her life.

LINDA P.

Targeted Muscle: Integrity
Performance Barrier: Lack of follow-through
Desired Outcome: Reliability

RITUAL

Ask two key questions before making a
  commitment
Add commitments I make to my to-do list
  with completion date

Married with an eight-year-old daughter, she worked most nights until 8:00 p.m., and often until 9 p.m. Her husband was self-employed, had a much more flexible schedule, and was effectively the primary parent. Linda didn't worry about her daughter's well-being, but she felt bereft about not seeing more of her. At work, meanwhile, she sensed a growing morale problem with her direct reports that baffled her.

Linda thought of herself as a model of integrity—someone who was trustworthy, fair, straightforward and caring. She took pride in trying always to do the right thing. She was stunned, therefore, to discover that the primary performance barrier cited by colleagues on her Full Engagement Inventory was that she was unreliable and couldn't be counted on to live up to her commitments.

We define integrity—a key ingredient in character and a primary spiritual muscle—as doing what you say you are going to do when you say you are going to do it. By this measure, Linda was perceived to fall considerably short. The key decisions for the department flowed through her, and her colleagues reported that she constantly made promises about getting work done that she failed to keep. Because Linda was so personally well liked and because her direct reports were aware how busy she was and how hard she worked, they were reluctant to hold her accountable. The result was that projects got backed up, leaving the people who worked for her feeling both frustrated and disempowered.

At first, Linda serenaded us with rationalizations: "I am incredibly busy, and I do the jobs of three people," and "I never make a promise that I don't intend to keep," and "I eventually get it all done, and when I don't, it's because the project really didn't merit a high priority in the first place." None of these explanations was likely to make the people who worked for her feel better, we pointed out, nor to solve the logjams she was creating. The simple truth was that Linda overestimated her capacity to efficiently meet the demands that she took on. That was what kept her at work late, left her feeling exhausted, and undermined her sense of connection with her family.

As Linda tried to understand her own behavior

better, she began to realize that it stemmed from a strong need for control and an unwillingness to trust others and to delegate. The fact that the people who worked for her felt resentful and frustrated was something that Linda found unacceptable. It was especially intolerable to think of herself as lacking integrity—a value that she put near the top of her list.

Linda created a simple ritual around commitment. Aware that her impulse was to take on every project put before her, she decided to institute a more structured, deliberate way of making such decisions. When any new challenge arose, she paused and asked herself two key questions. The first was "Is this something I need to do myself?" If her answer was yes, the second question was: "When does it need to be finished, and can I reasonably get it done by then?" If she had any doubt, she checked her calendar, and if she decided to take it on, she made an immediate addition to her to-do list, including a promised completion date.

"When I tell someone that I am going to do something, I make an absolute commitment, and I repeat it out loud," Linda told us later. "Very quickly I stopped making so many promises. I got better about prioritizing my time, and I began to delegate more of my responsibilities."

Giving up a certain amount of control raised difficult issues for Linda, and she continued to struggle with the feeling that if she didn't oversee key activities herself, they wouldn't get done right. At times, feeling frustrated, she took the job back into her own hands. Ultimately, however, she devised a solution to this impulse that was largely successful. She simply established very clear standards and objectives and held people accountable to them. Rather than take over a job herself when she wasn't satisfied with the result, she began giving it back to the responsible person to fix. Two very different kind of outcomes ensued. Two of her direct reports could not meet her standards, no matter how many times she sent jobs back. It finally dawned on her that they were the wrong people for their jobs and that she had been avoiding seeing this truth by taking over their work.

Linda decided to let one of the executives go and encouraged him to find work that better suited his talents. The other executive she reassigned to a job she believed was a far better fit. Sure enough, the executive began to excel. As for Linda's other direct reports, most of them palpably rose to the challenge of taking more responsibility and demonstrating a level of skill, creativity and initiative that exceeded Linda's expectations. "The truth is that my beginning to let go changed the atmosphere in my group," Linda told us. "People took much more ownership, the quality of our work improved, and I began leaving a lot earlier most nights."

MICHAEL D.: LACK OF TRUTHFULNESS, EXAGGERATION

If integrity has to do with reliably living up to our commitments, honesty is about telling the truth, to ourselves and to others. Both are key spiritual muscles. Michael D. is an investment adviser at a financial services company. He was sent to us by his boss late in 1999, along with other advisers in his division. Michael was annoyed to be pulled away from work for three days and skeptical that our program would be of much use to him. A top performer, he earned a very good income and rated himself very highly in nearly every category of our Full Engagement Inventory. Much of the feedback that he received from colleagues was likewise positive. Most rated him as highly focused, organized, friendly, optimistic and even-tempered.

The one area in which Michael received consistently low ratings was trustworthiness. He didn't find this entirely surprising, but it annoyed him. "They don't get it," he told us. "I'm much more honest about myself than they are. I admit who I am. I'm a salesman. I'm a promoter and a storyteller. My job is to get people excited about my products, to create positive spin. I don't sell stocks and bonds, I sell hope and promise. If I was a stickler with the facts, I'd never sell anything." He took a similar view about competing for clients. "People in the office will tell you I'm manipulative and tricky. The truth is I'm very straightforward. I

MICHAEL D.

Performance Barrier: Lack of truthfulness, exaggeration
Desired Outcome: Trustworthy
Targeted Muscle: Honesty

RITUAL

Monitor for exaggerations
Hold self accountable by correcting any misstatement

do what it takes to get clients, and then I do very well for them."

Michael had built a very successful practice through the 1990s based on his willingness to make big, bold bets, especially on technology stocks, with the wind of a bull market behind him. As far as Michael was concerned, his continuing success was his best defense. "I deliver the goods," he said, and he found very little of our program useful beyond the information about how to expand his physical capacity. Six months later, in mid-2000, Michael returned to us with his fellow financial advisers for the second stage of our training. At first, we were surprised to see him at all. It turned out that he was in a very different place. Three months earlier, the dot com crash had begun, and the stock market—most notably the NASDAQ—had dropped precipitously.

When technology stocks went into freefall, several of Michael's biggest bets plummeted in value. His own portfolio took a beating and so did his performance for his clients. The experience was both humbling and sobering, and it caused Michael to do some soul searching. He had, he realized, gotten caught up in his own hype, allowing himself to believe that the future was limitless. As the market plummeted, he was forced to step back and take time to reflect. He found that he could no longer kid himself. It had been the Emperor's new clothes all along, he concluded, and he was convinced that the market was headed significantly further down.

Michael spent a good deal of his time during his second visit wrestling with the issue of how to proceed with his clients. So long as he was making a lot of money for himself and for them, Michael didn't worry much about overstating or exaggerating or shaving the truth here and there. The fact that his clients were now suffering by virtue of his recommendations made him feel deeply uneasy. In the end, he decided that he didn't feel comfortable encouraging them to hold on, much less to make new investments in the market. Telling the truth—at least the truth as he now saw it—seemed like the only way to stop the damage and to feel comfortable with himself, even if that meant losing clients.

Specifically, Michael decided to sell a significant percentage of his holdings and take the losses, and to maintain a large cash position for the near term. He also resolved to speak personally with each of his clients to explain his decision, and to try to address their concerns as honestly as he could. Finally, he launched a very simple ritual to address the issue of trustworthiness. His instinct for exaggeration was so great that he often did it reflexively—doubling a projected number, or overstating the progress of a deal, or simply dressing up his comments with superlatives. The ritual that he introduced addressed accountability. Whenever Michael made a statement to a client or to a colleague, he determined to take a moment afterward to monitor his own accuracy. He was amazed to discover how frequently inaccurate information seemed to emerge from his lips. It made him feel like Jim Carrey in *Liar, Liar*.

Michael's second commitment was to correct himself as quickly as possible when he caught himself exaggerating, no matter how embarrassing that might be. He was relieved to discover that increasing his awareness and holding himself accountable had a huge impact on his behavior. After correcting himself a half-dozen times during the first couple of weeks of his ritual, he found that he was able to catch himself in most instances before he actually said something inaccurate. Within a month, speaking the truth had become more reflexive.

A few of Michael's clients did decide to move their business elsewhere, but the overwhelming majority stayed put. Michael's earnings diminished significantly and so, for a time, did his reputation in his firm. But over the course of the next eighteen months, the value of the stocks that he had sold early in 2000 continued to decline precipitously, along with the rest of the market. Many of his fellow investment advisers suffered huge losses, for themselves and their clients, while Michael's conservative portfolio held its own. His relationships with his clients grew closer. Many of them felt deeply appreciative that his decision had saved them from far more considerable losses, and they were also moved by his concern for their welfare. By mid-2001, Michael's client list had actually grown, largely from referrals, and his passion for what he was doing was higher than it had been at the height of the bull market. For the first time, he felt that he was genuinely serving clients rather than simply trying to maximize his earnings.

BEAR IN MIND

- Spiritual energy provides the force for action in all dimensions of our lives. It fuels passion, perseverance and commitment.
- Spiritual energy is derived from a connection to deeply held values and a purpose beyond our self-interest.
- Character—the courage and conviction to live by our deepest values—is the key muscle that serves spiritual energy.

- The key supportive spiritual muscles are passion, commitment, integrity and honesty.
- Spiritual energy expenditure and energy renewal are deeply interconnected.
- Spiritual energy is sustained by balancing a commitment to a purpose beyond ourselves with adequate self-care.
- Spiritual work can be demanding and renewing at the same time.
- Expanding spiritual capacity involves pushing past our comfort zone in precisely the same way that expanding physical capacity does.
- The energy of the human spirit can override even severe limitations of physical energy.

PART TWO

THE TRAINING SYSTEM

CHAPTER 8

DEFINING PURPOSE:
THE RULES
OF ENGAGEMENT

If growth and development take place from the bottom up—from physical to emotional to mental to spiritual—change is powered from the top down. The most compelling source of purpose is spiritual, the energy derived from connecting to deeply held values and a purpose beyond one's self-interest. Purpose creates a destination. It drives full engagement by prompting our desire to invest focused energy in a particular activity or goal. We become fully engaged only when we care deeply, when we feel that what we are doing really matters. Purpose is what lights us up, floats our boats, feeds our souls.

The search for meaning and purpose is among the most powerful and enduring themes in every culture since the origin of recorded history. It shows up in stories as early as Homer's *The Odyssey* and it has animated seekers as varied as

Jesus and the Buddha, Moses and Mohammed. The power of purpose is woven just as deeply through modern popular culture, in movies ranging from *Indiana Jones and the Last Crusade*, which retells the story of Perceval's search for the Holy Grail through the swashbuckling character of Indiana Jones; to the *Star Wars* trilogy, in which Luke Skywalker faces down his own deepest fears by overcoming Darth Vader and the Evil Empire and rescuing Princess Leia. It is no accident that these movies, deftly plying the archetypal themes of the search for meaning and the triumph of good over evil, are among the most successful of all time.

The philosopher and mythologist Joseph Campbell described the search for meaning and purpose as "The Hero's Journey." The basic elements of the path, he argued, recur across cultures and throughout history. Self-transformation, Campbell said, is our greatest challenge as human beings. The hero's journey begins when something awakens us to the need for change—illumination, discomfort, pain. Campbell described this as the "Call to Adventure." Once we accept the call, he said, we push forward into the unknown. Along the way we face doubt, uncertainty, fear and hardship. At some point, we realize that we cannot make the journey alone, and we seek help from a "mentor."

A series of tests push us to the brink of giving up, but in the "Supreme Ordeal" we finally slay the dragon—facing down the darkness within ourselves, calling on previously untapped potentials and creating meaning where it did not previously exist. We celebrate and acknowledge this accomplishment, but the process does not end there. Living out our purpose is a lifelong challenge. The journey continues and the true hero is always awaiting the next call to adventure. From the perspective of our program, the hero's journey is grounded in mobilizing, nurturing and regularly renewing our most precious resource— energy—in the service of what matters most. We are all facing extraordinary demands in extraordinary times. Few of us are satisfied to be ordinary—in our work, our marriages, as parents, as children to aging parents and as contributors to our communities. Ordinary is not enough. We want more from ourselves and others need more from us, whether it is our employers, our spouses, our children, our parents or our fellow citizens. In each of these situations, we want to be the best we can possibly be.

Unfortunately, most of us do not pursue the hero's path. The simple, almost embarrassing reality is that we feel too busy to search for meaning. Who has the time and the energy to actively pursue a deeper purpose? Instead, like Roger B., many of us sleepwalk through our lives, operating on automatic pilot most of the time. We meet our obligations but rarely question whether we could be reaching for something more. When we first asked Roger to describe what gave his life meaning, he hemmed and hawed and finally resorted to generalities and platitudes. "Taking care of my family," he said, and "being successful in my work." The truth, Roger acknowledged, was that he simply didn't feel any passion about anything.

Several years ago, the city of Orlando, Florida, planted a long line of trees along the highway that leads to our training center. The first time there was a storm with heavy winds, nearly every tree was blown down. The city dutifully sent workers to prop the trees back up. They secured them with baling wire and other external sources of support. It did no good. When the next storm came, the trees were blown over again. Over the next year, the same scenario repeated itself a half dozen times, despite a series of strategies to prop the trees back up.

It never seemed to occur to the folks in charge that if trees are to survive in a high-wind area, they must have a deeper root structure. It did occur to us that we were observing in nature a phenomenon that characterizes many of our own lives. Because we so often lack deep roots—firm beliefs and compelling values—we are easily buffeted by the prevailing winds. If we lack a strong sense of purpose we cannot hold our ground when we are challenged by life's inevitable storms. Instead, like Roger, we react defensively, blaming the storm or simply disengaging and ceasing to invest our energy. "You can work long hours but still be slothful," writes Joanne Ciulla, author of *The Working Life*. "The things that keep us from finding meaning are failure to actively engage in life and a certain laziness or lack of caring that allows us to let others make our decisions and tell us what things mean."

MEASURING THE POWER OF PURPOSE

Purpose is a unique source of energy and power. As we suggested earlier, it fuels focus, direction, passion and perseverance. To get a quick sense of the power of your own purpose, take out your pen and paper and spend a few moments answering the following three questions, using a scale of 1 to 10.

- How excited are you to get to work in the morning?
- How much do you enjoy what you do for its own sake rather than for what it gets you?
- How accountable do you hold yourself to a deeply held set of values?

If the answers to these questions total 27 or more, it suggests that you already bring a significant sense of purpose to what you do. If your answers fall below 22, you are more likely going through the motions. The issue is not so much whether your life is providing you with a sense of meaning as it is whether you are actively using life as a vehicle through which to express your deepest values. As Viktor Frankl puts it: "Ultimately, man should not ask what the meaning of his life is, but rather he must recognize that it is he who is asked. In a word, each man is questioned by life; and he can only answer to life by answering for his own life; to life he can only respond by being responsible."

There are many levels of spiritual development, much as there are sequential levels of physical, emotional and mental development. Religion professor Wade Roofs has defined spirituality as "knowing our deepest selves and what is sacred to us." We start at this most basic level because we have found that it has both universality and great utility. Powerful transformations occur for our clients when they are able to shift their focus from filling deficits to cultivating deeper values and defining a vision for themselves. As the tennis player Arthur Ashe once put it: "From what we get in life, we make a living. From what we give, we make a life."

When Andy L. came to see us late in 2001, he had lost his way. The president and CEO of a large real estate development company, he felt completely disengaged at work. "I had been through a series of health challenges, and the medication regime had left me feeling bloated and sluggish," he explained, "but really these were symptoms of something bigger. For nearly all my life, I felt passionate about my work. Then I ran into some difficult management issues, and I had some frustrating setbacks. It got to the point that I didn't even care about getting up to go to work in the morning. I was deep into victim mode and I needed a lifeline."

Defining what mattered to him most created a breakthrough for Andy. He settled on five key values—persistence, integrity, excellence, reativity and commitment. They became his touchstone—and the source of his motivation for change.

"All day, every day, whether I'm at work or I'm exercising or I'm with my family, I ask myself if what I'm doing is serving my values," Andy explains. "If my motivation for exercising hard had been fitting into the pants that I wore two years ago, that would have worked for a while, but it wouldn't have lasted. When I'm on the treadmill now and I feel like getting off, what I think about is persistence, integrity and commitment. Without linking up to those values, I'd be asking myself "Why the hell am I doing this?" and I'd probably quit. Andy brings a similar thought process to his eating habits. In the first two months after working with us, he lost thirty-two pounds. Between working out and losing weight, his energy increased dramatically.

Andy called on the fuel of purpose very directly at work. "When I'm on the job," he explains, "I'm asking myself 'Am I generating the kind of leadership, providing direction, setting strategy and responding to the marketplace in a way that is reflective of my five key values?' For me the values create a very simple mirror. They keep me on purpose, and they renew me when I find myself wandering off course. My sense of commitment is way up, and I'm communicating that energy to others. I'm leaping out of bed in the mornings. I have absolutely retaken responsibility for the results of my company. I'm leading with purpose, which I wasn't doing before."

POSITIVE PURPOSE

Purpose becomes a more powerful and enduring source of energy in our lives in three ways: when its source moves from negative to positive, external to internal and self to others.

A negative source of purpose is defensive and deficit-based. It arises in the face of threat—physical or psychological. When we feel our security and survival are at stake, emotions such as fear, anger and even hatred can be a powerful source of energy. The problem is the cost. As we saw earlier, negative emotions drain energy and prompt the release of hormones that are toxic to our systems over time.

Purpose fueled by the feeling of deficit also narrows our attention and limits our possibilities. Imagine, for a moment, that you are out on the sea in a boat that springs a leak. Your purpose immediately becomes mobilized around keeping the boat from sinking. But so long as you are busy bailing water, you can't navigate towards a destination. The same is true in our lives. When we are preoccupied with filling our own holes to stay afloat, we have little energy available to define any deeper or more enduring purpose. By contrast, when we are able to move from the inner experience of threat to one of challenge, we introduce a whole new range of possibilities into our lives. Rather than reacting to fear, we can focus on what moves us and feels meaningful.

Janet R. is a highly driven senior executive at a large New York City media company. By her own description, she brought to her work a fierce commitment to excellence. She saw this as a primary value in her life, and she felt that it had helped her to rise steadily up the corporate ladder. As with Roger B., a somewhat different picture emerged when we began to look beneath the surface in her life. The feedback Janet received from colleagues on her Full Engagement Inventory indicated that while they did indeed see her as committed, focused and intelligent, they also found her to be highly controlling and defensive.

Janet found this feedback painful but also provocative. She had always assumed that she derived purpose from her commitment to excellence. At the same time, she acknowledged that she took very little pleasure in work well done. At best, she felt a brief sense of relief and then a renewed anxiety about the next challenge. What really drove her, she realized, was a fierce hunger to avoid mistakes. Even small ones, she said, made her feel vulnerable to criticism—her own and that of others. The consequence was that Janet lived in a state of narrowly focused attention, forever zeroing in on the potential for failure. Physically, the toll showed up in headaches and lower back pain. Emotionally, Janet lived in a state of tension that robbed her of energy and enthusiasm, and antagonized her colleagues. Mentally, her obsession with getting everything right compromised her willingness to take risks and to exercise much creativity.

As Janet explored her motivation more deeply, she realized that she had turned her commitment to excellence into a form of tyranny, and that her perfectionism had a devastating energy consequence—in her own life and on others. When she began to explore her values more deeply, she realized that she especially admired kindness and humility in others and wished that she could better embody these qualities in her own life.

Janet decided to institute a ritual of revisiting her primary values every morning. By learning to balance a continuing positive passion for excellence with a newfound commitment to humility and concern for others, she began to tap into a more positive and less costly source of spiritual energy.

"I started to see how much I viewed the world as an enemy I was always fighting against," Janet told us. "It also occurred to me that I didn't always have all the answers. Changing my outlook has been one of the toughest challenges I've ever taken on, but connecting to the values of kindness and humility has been like taking a close friend along on the journey. I still don't like being wrong, but I see now that's it's not the end of the world. Sometimes it's more important to stay connected with people than to be right."

INTRINSIC PURPOSE

Purpose also becomes a more powerful source of energy when it moves from being externally to internally motivated. Extrinsic motivation reflects the desire to get more of something that we don't feel we have enough of: money, approval, social standing, power or even love. "Intrinsic" motivation grows out of the desire to engage in an activity because we value it for the inherent satisfaction it provides. Researchers have long found that intrinsic motivation tends to prompt more sustaining energy. A study conducted by the University of Rochester's Human Motivation Research Group found, for example, that people whose motivation was authentic—defined as "self-authored"—exhibited more interest, excitement and confidence, as well as greater persistence, creativity and performance than a control group of subjects who were motivated largely by external demands and rewards.

Nowhere are the limits of an external source of purpose so clear as with money. While money serves as a primary source of motivation and an ongoing preoccupation for many of us, researchers have found almost no correlation between income levels and happiness. Between 1957 and 1990, per person income in the United States doubled, taking into account inflation. Not only did people's reported levels of happiness fail to increase at all during the same period, but rates of depression grow nearly tenfold. The incidence of divorce, suicide, alcoholism and drug abuse also rose dramatically.

"We humans need food, rest, warmth and social contact," writes David Myers, author of *The Pursuit of Happiness*. "For starving Sudanese and homeless Iraqis money would buy more happiness. But having more than enough provides little additional boost to well being. . . . Once we're comfortable, more money therefore provides diminishing returns. . . . The correlation between income and happiness is modest, and in both the U.S. and Canada [it] has now dropped to near zero. . . . Income also doesn't noticeably influence satisfaction with marriage, family, friendship or ourselves— all of which do predict a sense of well being." Happiness, in turn, has been clearly associated with higher productivity. In short, money may not buy happiness, but happiness may help you get rich.

Extrinsic rewards have actually been shown to undermine intrinsic motivation. Researchers

Mark R. Lepper and David R. Green spent time watching nursery school children at play in order to assess what they most enjoyed doing. Next, they began giving each child a reward each time he or she engaged in the preferred activity. Across the board, the children's interest in activities quickly diminished when they were associated with rewards. In a second study, adults doing puzzles were rewarded each time they were successful in completing them. Like the children, their interest in continuing the activity progressively decreased. Plainly, people can be motivated by material gain and by external praise. The point is that we feel more passion for and derive more pleasure from doing what we freely choose and most enjoy.

James D. was a senior executive in corporate communications for more than twenty years. He was well paid, and his job had allowed him and his wife to buy a large house that they loved, to live very comfortably, to take luxurious vacations and to put their three children through private school. James found his work intellectually challenging, but he never felt inspired or excited by it. The rewards he derived were almost all external. As he moved into his late forties, he hungered for something more. When he began to define his purpose, it became clear that what gave him the deepest sense of satisfaction was teaching—and learning. His happiest memories were from college and graduate school, when he pursued learning for its own sake.

The first change that James made was to get a part-time position teaching a communications course at a local university without giving up his day job. Six months later, he was offered the opportunity to take over the university's public information department, while continuing to teach there. It meant taking a pay cut of more than 60 percent, but James didn't hesitate. He quit his corporate job. By this point, his wife had decided to return to work herself, and that helped to ease the loss of income.

For the first year, James took on an occasional freelance consulting job to supplement their income, and they dipped into savings to cover the difference between their costs and their expenses. In the second year, without even thinking much about it, they began to cut back, especially on luxuries, and James gave up the freelancing, which he had done only halfheartedly.

During his corporate career, James had spent considerable time worrying about money, even as his income steadily increased. In his new life he found that he spent very little time thinking about money at all. With their two youngest kids in college, he and his wife decided to sell their large house, move into a smaller one and cut their expenses still further. James spent fewer hours actually working at his new job than he had in his corporate life. Nonetheless, fueled by a passionate sense of purpose, he was far more efficient and productive than he had ever been before. He also found that he had time to begin a part-time graduate program in history, an interest that he had given up in college as unlikely to lead to a good living. One of the perks of his new job was the opportunity to take courses at no cost.

A PURPOSE BEYOND ONE'S SELF

The third factor that ignites a deeper sense of purpose is shifting attention from fulfilling our own needs and desires to serving something beyond ourselves. Undeniably, people will work hard to get rich or famous or to win more admiration. But to what lengths will they go to achieve such goals? It is not uncommon for people to put their lives at risk in the service of causes they deeply believe in. Soldiers do so regularly in war. New York City firemen did so when they entered the towers of the World Trade Center in the aftermath of the terrorist attacks on 9/11. Just think for a moment about a doctor who is motivated primarily by money, compared with one whose sense of purpose comes from the desire to be a healer and to serve his patients with excellence. The doctor who is looking to maximize his income might make very different decisions than one whose primary focus is the quality of the care that he provides to patients. Given equal skills, which one would you prefer to have care for you in a life-or-death situation?

"Work makes life better," writes Joanne Ciulla,

author of *The Working Life*, "if it helps others; alleviates suffering; eliminates difficult or tedious toil; makes someone healthier and happier; or aesthetically or intellectually enriches people and improves the environment in which we live." Many of our clients blame their work environments for their unhappiness and their absence of passion. But it is not necessarily the nature of the job that determines how meaningful and motivating it is. The challenge we all face is to find ways to use the workplace as a forum in which to express and embody our deepest values. We can derive a sense of purpose, for example, from mentoring others, or being part of a cohesive team, or simply from a commitment to treating others with respect and care and from communicating positive energy. The real measure of our lives may ultimately be in the small choices we make in each and every moment.

Clarifying purpose takes time—quiet, uninterrupted time—which is something that many of us feel we simply do not have. We are forever rushing from one obligation to the next without any larger sense of direction. It seems almost self-indulgent to spend time on questions of meaning and purpose. It may help to think of energy devoted to these issues as an investment with the potential to deliver a high return over time—increased energy, fuller engagement, higher productivity and greater satisfaction.

So long as we skim across the surface of our lives at high speeds, it is impossible to dig down more deeply. People cannot move horizontally and vertically at the same time. When clients come through our program, one of our aims is to help them slow down, to put aside their preoccupations and their pressing demands for long enough to step back and take a look at the choices they are making. It is no coincidence that every enduring spiritual tradition has emphasized practices such as prayer, retreat, contemplation and meditation—all means by which to quietly connect with and regularly revisit what matters most. You might begin your own inquiry very simply by giving some thought to the following question: "Is the life I am living worth what I am giving up to have it?"

VALUES AND VIRTUES

Deeply held values fuel the energy on which purpose is built. They define an enduring code of conduct—the rules of engagement in the journey to bring our vision for ourselves to life. The pursuit of power or wealth or fame may all be a sources of motivation, but these goals are external and often fill deficiency needs rather than serving growth and transformation. We may value crushing our enemies, or amassing more money than our neighbors, or achieving social standing and prestige. But these are not values as we define them in our work with clients. Values, we believe, have intrinsic worth. They provide a source of inspiration and meaning that cannot be taken away from us.

Across cultures, religions and time itself, people have admired and aspired to the same universal values—among them integrity, generosity, courage, humility, compassion, loyalty, perseverance—while rejecting their opposites—deceit, greed, cowardice, arrogance, callousness, disloyalty and sloth. To begin to explore more deeply the values that are most compelling to you, we suggest that you set aside uninterrupted time to respond to the following questions:

• Jump ahead to the end of your life. What are the three most important lessons you have learned and why are they so critical?
• Think of someone that you deeply respect. Describe three qualities in this person that you most admire.
• Who are you at your best?
• What one-sentence inscription would you like to see on your tombstone that would capture who you really were in your life?

Each of these questions is a means of surfacing the values that will define your "rules of engagement" in whatever mission you are on. What matters most to you will be revealed in the life lessons that you consider most important, in the qualities that you most admire in another person, and perhaps above all in your description of who you are at your best. The accompanying Deepest Values Checklist includes a list of commonly held values. It is simply a set of suggestions. Add to it any other values that you consider important. Our goal is to help you begin to identify which ones are most motivating to you personally.

A value is ultimately just a roadmap for action. Values that we fail to reflect in our behavior are ultimately empty. To be meaningful, a value must influence the choices that we make in our everyday lives. Professing one set of beliefs and living by another is not just hypocritical, but also evidence of disconnection and misalignment. The more we are committed to and guided by our values, the more powerful a source of energy they become.

A value in action is a virtue.

We may hold generosity as a value, but the virtue is behaving generously. Alignment occurs when we transform our values into virtues. Simply identifying our primary values is not sufficient. The next step is to define more precisely how we intend to embody the values in our daily lives—regardless of external pressures. For example: "I demonstrate the value of generosity by investing energy in others, without expectation that I will receive anything in return, and by my willingness to put the agendas of those I care about ahead of my own, even if it means inconveniencing myself at times."

DEEPEST VALUES CHECKLIST

Authenticity

Balance

Commitment

Compassion

Concern for others

Courage

Creativity

Empathy

Excellence

Fairness

Faith

Family

Freedom

Friendship

Generosity

Genuineness

Happiness

Harmony

Health

Honesty

Humor

Integrity

Kindness

Knowledge

Loyalty

Openness

Perseverance

Respect for others

Responsibility

Security

Serenity

Service to others

Too often our motivation for a behavior is expedient rather than value driven. We do what makes us feel good in the moment or fills a hole or lessens our pain. If you are feeling anxious, the expedient energy choice may be to eat a chocolate chip cookie or smoke a cigarette or drink a couple of beers to salve the discomfort. If you are rushing to meet a pressing deadline for an important project, the expedient choice might be to raise your voice and order people around. If you make a mistake that is going to get you in trouble, you may disclaim responsibility and blame others.

Values hold us to a different standard for managing energy.

If you have identified self-care as a value, you may resist the lure of a cookie or a cigarette or a drink. If you value respect for others, you may feel impelled to exercise self-control even when you are under pressure. If you hold integrity as a key value, you will more likely take responsibility for a mistake even if it means incurring criticism. It is relatively easy to act in accord with our values when we are feeling comfortable and secure. The real test is when virtuous behavior demands that we resist instant gratification and make sacrifices. It is in these situations that values serve us best, both as a source of energy and as a code of conduct.

WALKING THE TALK

Think back for a moment to Barry F., the CEO who told us that respect for others was his primary value, but whose direct reports told us that he regularly kept them waiting. It was only when he connected his value to his behavior that he recognized the disconnection and felt compelled to make a change. Much the same was true for Michael D., the investment adviser who decided to take a stand and sell his positions, even at the risk of losing clients. Only when he identified integrity and concern for others as deep values in his life did he feel compelled to take action and change his long-standing behavior.

Values-based behavior doesn't invariably lead to greater financial rewards. Nonetheless Jim Collins makes a compelling case, in his book *Built to Last*, that values-driven companies do indeed perform better in the long run. Our own argument is simply that strongly held values drive fuller engagement in all arenas of our lives. Put another way, a values-driven life increases the likelihood that you will bring passion, commitment and perseverance to whatever it is you do.

Susan D. is an advertising executive who came to us complaining bitterly about her work environment and specifically about a boss whom she considered to be impossible to please. No matter what Susan accomplished, the boss gave her the feeling that it wasn't enough. Over time, Susan found herself slowly disengaging, working half-heartedly and being less productive. Why invest her heart and soul, she figured, when she saw no hope of being recognized or rewarded for her efforts? Frustration and resentment consumed much of her remaining energy and the downward spiral fed on itself. As her performance suffered, she felt worse about herself. The worse that she felt, the more distracted she became.

The problem, we helped Susan to see, was that she had defined her value purely in external terms. So long as she invested energy primarily in winning her boss's approval, she was doomed to disappointment. When she turned inward and began to explore her own deepest values, Susan found two that were especially compelling: excellence and commitment. By holding herself accountable to behaving in accord with these values she began to feel better about herself, more aligned, and more engaged. Susan remained unhappy to be in a workplace in which she felt unappreciated. But with refocused energy, her performance improved, her spirits rose and she began to look for a new job. Within two months, she located a position in a different part of the company working for a boss she liked and found inspiring.

It is not always that easy. There are times when we must endure difficult bosses and stressful work environments. Even then, when we are guided by clear values, we can continue to make choices about how to behave from a position of confidence, strength and dignity rather than from anger, resentment and insecurity. In some cases, it may make sense to change our circumstances. But challenges and difficulties never disappear. In the end, we must live in concert with our values wherever we find ourselves.

A VISION OF FULL ENGAGEMENT

The next step in defining purpose is to create a vision for how we intend to invest our energy. A compelling vision statement strikes a careful balance. On the one hand, in order to provide inspiration it needs to be lofty, ambitious and even a bit overreaching. On the other hand, in order to have teeth it needs to be realistic, specific and personal. We give clients an opportunity to write both a personal and a professional vision statement, although many choose to create a single document that covers both. Either way, defining a vision becomes a picture of the possible, a blueprint for action, and a buffer against the inclination to make energy choices reactively rather than reflectively.

Sara J. is the forty-nine-year-old president of a small consulting company. She began by identifying six core values: integrity, respect for others, excellence, gratitude, self-care and service to others. Next, she got more specific about what these values meant to her in practical, everyday terms. She defined integrity, for example, as "matching my behaviors to my promises, holding myself accountable and making amends as quickly as possible when I fall short." She embodied gratitude by "taking time out each day to appreciate and acknowledge the blessings and good fortune in my life and focusing on what is best in people and in my everyday experience." For Sara, living out the value of self-care meant "making my own health and happiness a priority by addressing my important needs and seeking regular renewal in all dimensions of my life."

Over a period of several months and multiple

drafts Sara created a vision statement, grounded in her primary values, that was a blend of inspiration and down-to-earth specificity:

Above all else I walk my talk, so that my behaviors reflect my values. I fight passionately for what I believe, but remain open to learning and growing. At work, I am committed to helping people grow, deepen and behave more effectively in the world. I treat all people in my life with respect, kindness and consideration.

In my personal life, I appreciate, enjoy and give generously to my husband and children, the members of my extended family and my closest friends. I also take care of myself, not just physically but also emotionally, mentally and spiritually.

Whatever happens, I am grateful for all that I have been given. Serving others is both a responsibility and a privilege.

A vision statement is a declaration of intent about how to invest one's energy. Regularly revisited, it serves as a source of sustaining direction and a fuel for action. For Vince K., an executive in charge of traders on the New York Stock Exchange, changing his energy management habits both at work and at home proved to be a turning point in his life. "Connecting to my core values was instrumental in refocusing my energies," he explains. "I was pretty strung out and the whole process of defining my purpose was the catalyst for realizing that I needed to reengage with my family. That was my number one value. It's easy to give lip service to being a good husband and a good parent. Through the self-evaluation process, I realized the importance of really committing my energy to what I care about on a day-to-day basis. That required giving up drinking, because it was impossible to truly be with my wife and my kids if I drank. It also meant getting back into shape, which was a way to handle the pressures of work better and have more energy when I was at home. Quitting drinking, working out regularly and recommitting to my family changed my whole attitude about life. It made me a better husband, a better father and a better boss."

BEAR IN MIND

- The search for meaning is among the most powerful and enduring themes in every culture since the origin of recorded history.
- The "hero's journey" is grounded in mobilizing, nurturing and regularly renewing our most precious resource—energy—in the service of what matters most.
- When we lack a strong sense of purpose we are easily buffeted by life's inevitable storms.
- Purpose becomes a more powerful and enduring source of energy when its source moves from

negative to positive, external to internal and self to others.

- A negative source of purpose is defensive and deficit-based.
- Intrinsic motivation grows out of the desire to engage in an activity because we value it for the inherent satisfaction it provides.
- Values fuel the energy on which purpose is built. They hold us to a different standard for managing our energy.
- A virtue is a value in action.
- A vision statement, grounded in values that are meaningful and compelling, creates a blueprint for how to invest our energy.

CHAPTER 9

FACE THE TRUTH:
HOW ARE YOU MANAGING
YOUR ENERGY NOW?

I t is one thing to clarify our values and quite another to behave in accordance with them each and every day. Facing the truth about the gap between who we want to be and who we really are is never easy. Each of us has an infinite capacity for self-deception. In myriad ways, we push from our awareness that which we find unpleasant or upsetting or contrary to the way we wish to see ourselves. Until we can clear away the smoke and mirrors and look honestly at ourselves, we have no starting point for change. The maverick psychiatrist R. D. Laing captured this cleverly in a short poem:

> The range of what we think and do
> Is limited by what we fail to notice
> And because we fail to notice
> That we fail to notice

There is little we can do
To change
Until we notice
How failing to notice
Shapes our thoughts and deeds

In previous chapters we have argued that full engagement and optimal performance depend on the capacity to marshal high positive energy. Facing painful truths brings up more unpleasant and uncomfortable feelings including guilt, anger, frustration, envy, sadness, greed and insecurity. As in all dimensions of our lives, there is a tension between the opposites here. When it comes to engaging in the world, high positive energy clearly serves us best. To perform optimally, we must learn to set aside negative feelings. But when avoiding painful truths becomes a way of life, we eventually suffer the consequences. Denial is akin to holding a finger in the dike. The pressure of suppressing feelings will eventually be too great, and the toll will show up somewhere—in anxiety, depression or numbness, diminished performance on the job, a marriage that blows up, even physical illness.

There are times, of course, when our capacity to deny reality serves us well. When Lauren Manning was severely burned by a fireball following the attack on Two World Trade Center, she felt no immediate pain. Had she experienced the full brunt of her injuries, she almost certainly would have collapsed and died. Instead, she somehow managed to escape the building moments before it came down. But pain is also a signal that something is wrong. Within moments of Manning's escape, her injuries became almost unbearable, and she was rushed to the hospital with severe burns across 40 percent of her body. Attending to her pain the minute that she was out of imminent danger proved just as critical to saving her life as ignoring it earlier.

Often, however, we respond to less life-threatening forms of pain in our everyday lives much the way that Manning did. We instinctively shut them out of consciousness. The costs surface when our denial becomes a permanent solution. Unpleasant facts don't go away simply because we stop paying conscious attention to them.

Denial is effectively a form of disengagement: It means shutting down a part of ourselves. When we fear the truth, we become more defensive, rigid and constricted. Like an anesthetic, avoiding the truth numbs us from pain, but it also cuts us off from freely and fully engaging in the world. In addition, denial and self-deception require energy, which is then no longer available for more productive activities. Happily, the opposite is also true. Opening to the truth about ourselves creates freedom. "Whatever is flexible and flowing will tend to grow," says the Tao Te Ching.

Facing the truth also gives us an opportunity to understand and address negative feelings rather than inadvertently acting them out. We will inevitably fall short and even violate our values at times. But rather than denying our shortcomings and missteps, by acknowledging them we can learn from them. To be effective in the world, we must find a balance between looking honestly at the most painful truths and contradictions in our lives and engaging in the world with hope and positive energy. From an energy perspective, it is easy to be negative. Optimism requires courage, not just because life itself is finite, but also because we all inevitably face challenges, obstacles and setbacks along the way.

Take the extreme experience of losing someone close to you. If you override and deny feelings of grief, difficult and upsetting as they may be, they tend to fester inside and take a toll over time. Similarly, if you wallow in despair without seeking to slowly reengage in the world, feelings of loss and sadness can become paralyzing and self-reinforcing. Grief, like most toxic emotions, is best metabolized in waves, intermittently opening up the energy channel to allow the sadness in and then seeking recovery in the form of comfort, laughter, hope and reengagement.

There are times—not just in emergencies—when consciously choosing not to pay attention to real information serves a useful purpose. An athlete can be successful competing, for example, only when she focuses her attention fully on the task at hand. Doing so may require temporarily shutting out genuine worries about her family, or a nagging pain in her knee, or even a lack of confidence in her skills. The same capacity to set aside potential distractions is necessary to be successful in our own work lives. Setting aside our anxieties and pre-occupations is healthy when it represents a choice rather than a compulsion, a means of more fully engaging in the task at hand rather than an unconscious strategy to avoid discomfort. Selective inattention doesn't necessarily mean denying or avoiding troubling issues. Instead it may be a strategy for putting them on hold in order to deal with them at a more appropriate time.

More often, self-deception is unconscious and provides short-term relief while prompting long-term costs. At the most basic level, we deceive ourselves in order to protect our self-esteem—our image of who we are or wish to be. To keep at bay the truths that we find most painful and unacceptable—most notably the places in our lives where our behavior conflicts with our deepest values—we use a range of strategies. Drugs and alcohol can temporarily blot out uncomfortable feelings and provide the illusion of well being. So, in a similar way, do overeating, casual sex, and even seemingly benign addictions such as workaholism and service to others. "Every form of addiction is bad," wrote Carl Jung, "no matter whether the narcotic be alcohol or morphine or idealism."

THE DEFENSE DEPARTMENT

We each also have our own well-funded defense departments. Numbing out—simply not feeling much of anything no matter how objectively disturbing it may be—is one form of denial. Think about a deteriorating marriage, in which one partner (and sometimes both) reacts by withdrawing emotional energy rather than facing difficult issues. Rationalization is another common defense against the truth. A client of ours might acknowledge feedback that he is rude to others or impatient or critical, but in the next breath ascribe it to a seemingly honorable motive such as the need to get a job done quickly.

Intellectualizing is a means of acknowledging a truth cognitively without experiencing its impact emotionally. A graphic example is the leader who charismatically makes the case for honesty, or decency, or teamwork to his gathered troops, only to flagrantly violate his professed principles in his everyday conduct. Projection is an especially insidious defense against facing the truth—one that often lies at the heart of evil. It involves attributing one's own unacknowledged impulses to others. We often see anger or hatred or arrogance or greed in those around us, rather than fully owning these same feelings in ourselves.

Imagining the worst in every situation is a means of distorting the truth by perceiving it through a narrowly pessimistic lens. "Somatizing" is the conversion of unacknowledged anxiety and anger into physical symptoms—headaches, digestive problems, back and neck pain. The Woody Allen joke "I don't get angry, I grow a tumor" carries a considerable dollop of truth. We are far more likely to elicit sympathy from others for our back pain or our migraines than for our anxiety and our pessimism. Sublimation—channeling an unacceptable feeling such as greediness into excessive generosity—represents a more positively adaptive defense. Even then, the underlying negative impulse is left in place, strongly felt but fiercely denied.

Looking honestly at our own behavior is only the first step. It is equally important to take responsibility for the choices that we make. The truth may set you free, but it won't take you where you need to go. For example, it is a positive step for a client to acknowledge that he is twenty-five pounds over his ideal weight—not five or ten as he may initially claim—but it is also easy to dismiss the importance of its truth. "I feel fine, so what's the big deal?" he might say, or "Almost everyone I know is a little overweight," or "I'm just stressed right now and I'll deal with it later." The challenge is not just to acknowledge the fact of being overweight, but also to face the truth about its consequences—compromised energy, a much higher likelihood of diabetes and heart disease and a far greater likelihood of early death. Only when we face these truths and act upon them do we fully embrace the truth. The chart on pages 154–155 depicts the costs and benefits of ten of the most common expedient behaviors that we see among our clients. In each case, we note its short-term costs and its benefits, as well as its likely long-term consequences.

THE SHADOW SELF

Carl Jung coined the term "shadow" to describe those aspects of ourselves that we split off because they violate our self-image. Freud characterized repression as the means by which we exile unwanted feelings into our unconscious. In Buddhism, the form of meditation known as Vipassana aims at overcoming our instinct for delusion by learning to see things exactly as they are. Whatever we fail to notice and acknowledge, we tend to act out. If expressing anger was deemed unacceptable as we grew up and doing so now violates our self-image, we may express it covertly by being critical and judgmental or stubborn or chronically resentful. When we have blind spots, we can blindside others without even being aware that we are doing so.

Frightened by an underlying feeling of power-lessness, the bully compensates by treating people harshly. Haunted by unacknowledged feelings of inadequacy, the successful executive forever parades his achievements and talks endlessly about the famous and important people he knows.

Unable to face her own underlying envy, the polite and proper hostess finds subtle ways to disparage and dismiss everyone around her. "The central defect of evil is not the sin but the refusal to acknowledge it," writes M. Scott Peck, author of *The Road Less Traveled.* "The evil attack others instead of facing their own failures . . . since they must deny their own badness, they must perceive others as bad."

The opposite may also be true. Trapped in a narrow vision of ourselves, we may also fail to notice and nurture our hidden strengths. Much as we suppress that which we find distasteful in ourselves, so we may fail to give ourselves credit for our best qualities. To face the truth also means acknowledging and celebrating our strengths.

For millennia, sages have understood that the ultimate spiritual challenge is to "wake up." In classical times, the Greeks wrote two exhortations into the side of Mount Parnassus. "Know Thyself" is the most celebrated. The second translates roughly as "Know All of Thyself"—a recognition that we must look beneath the surface to find the truth. Other modern thinkers have echoed this message. "It is not until we have truly been shocked into seeing ourselves as we really are," writes psychiatrist Edward Whitmont, "instead of as we wish or hopefully assume we are, that we can take the first step toward individual reality."

WHAT WE FAIL TO NOTICE

When he first came to us, Roger B. thought of himself as honest and straightforward. His inclination, however, was to put a positive spin on his own experience. This, we find, is very common. In the face of relentless demand, we become so acclimated to a chronic state of mild anxiety and moderate discontent that we accept it as the status quo and forget what it's like to feel any differently. Alternatively, we go into denial or numbness, insisting that things are fine, even when our expedient choices are undeniably self-destructive in the long term.

In the course of our work—and with the help of feedback from his colleagues—Roger discovered a range of strategies that he used to deny or avoid taking responsibility for the more unpleasant and unacceptable aspects of his life. Blaming others and seeing himself as a victim was a big one. He attributed his troubles at work largely to the lack of attention from his boss and to the economic environment. He cited time pressures beyond his control as the explanation for why he didn't exercise, or eat well, or spend much time with his kids.

Roger was also deft at rationalizing his unhealthy behaviors, aided by a dose of self-deception. We call this the "not dead yet" syndrome. What is the big deal, Roger told himself, about smoking a few cigarettes a week (it eventually emerged that the

CONFRONTING THE COSTS AND BENEFITS

Expedient Adaptation	Benefit Now
Pessimistic attitude	Less disappointment, less risk, less vulnerability
Poor work/life balance (long hours, limited time for family and friends)	Accomplish more at work; less emotional risk, avoid responsibilities outside of work
Anger and impatience	Prompts action; discharges tension
Numbing out	Reduces pain and stress
Poor stress-recovery balance (failure to oscillate)	Accomplish more short-term; productive
Multitasking (e.g., answer email while talking on the phone)	Get more tasks accomplished; feel productive; high excitement
Poor diet (high fat, high sugar)	Immediate gratification; convenience
Defensiveness with co-workers	Keeps people at a safe distance, avoids responsibility
Excessive alcohol and drug use	Immediate pleasure; reduced tension and anxiety; greater social ease
No exercise	More time for work and other obligations, less effort

Cost	Long-Term Consequences
Reduced positive energy, interpersonal effectiveness, happiness	Reduced performance, health, happiness
Lack of time for intimate connection; resentment of family and friends	Unfulfilling relationships; tendency to impatience and anger; burnout; regret; guilt; and loss of passion
Antagonizes colleagues; begets more anger	Demotivating and antagonizing to others; undermines close relationships; increases health risks
Reduces passion, connection to others	Shallow life; lack of meaning; reduced performance
Fatigue, reduced passion and performance, higher health risks	Reduced health; higher rate of burnout; undermines relationships, diminishes performance
Divided attention; less fully engaged with people; lower quality of work	Shallowness of connection to others; less capacity for absorbed attention; lower quality of work
High cholesterol; increased weight, less sustained high positive energy	Increased risk of obesity, heart disease, stroke, cancer and early death
Alienates co-workers; undermines teamwork; impedes learning	Isolation; rigidity; poor relationships; failure to grow and improve quality of work
Impaired concentration; erratic work performance; mood swings; troubled relationships	Higher health risks; undermines relationships self-esteem and performance
Less energy, strength, general well-being; lost source of recovery from mental activities more susceptibility to sickness	Undermines health, lowers concentration and access to high positive energy; increases chances of early death

241

number was closer to a dozen), or having a couple of drinks at the end of the long day (with clients it often became three or four) or putting on a few extra pounds (assuming that twenty pounds still counts as "a few"). When Roger felt guilty about some behavior or overwhelmed by his circumstances, he tended to go to the other extreme. He would paint such a bleak, self-disparaging picture of himself that within a short time all he wanted was some way to push away the discomfort—and thus the cycle of self-deception resumed. Above all others, denial was his drug of choice.

Roger's strategies were scarcely the most extreme that we have encountered. A respiratory therapist we know—someone who worked in hospitals with patients who had emphysema and other similar illnesses—was diagnosed recently with lung cancer. It turned out that she had been a smoker for twenty years. Extraordinary as it seems, she had managed to willfully resist tying her own behavior to the horrifying consequences of smoking that she had observed at work every day for more than a decade.

When Tony moderated a panel at a conference on emotional intelligence several years ago, one of the panelists was an academic psychologist who had been a pioneer in the field. "Give us an example," Tony asked each panelist, "of a way that you have increased your emotional intelligence during the past year." The psychologist was stumped. "It's really difficult," he said sheepishly.

"There really isn't much support for developing emotional intelligence in the academic world."

GATHERING THE FACTS

Facing the truth requires making yourself the object of inquiry—conducting an audit of your life and holding yourself accountable for the energy consequences of your behaviors. To get a quick overview, take out a piece of paper and a pen and set aside at least thirty quiet minutes to answer this series of questions:

- On a scale of 1 to 10, how fully engaged are you in your work? What is standing in your way?
- How closely does your everyday behavior match your values and serve your mission? Where are the disconnects?
- How fully are you embodying your values and vision for yourself at work? At home? In your community? Where you are falling short?
- How effectively are the choices that you are making physically—your habits of nutrition, exercise, sleep and the balance of stress and recovery—serving your key values?
- How consistent with your values is your emotional response in any given situation? Is it different at work than it is at home, and if so, how?
- To what degree do you establish clear priorities and sustain attention to tasks? How consistent

are those priorities with what you say is most important to you?

Now take this inquiry one step further, and make it more open-ended. If energy is your most precious resource, let's look at how well you manage it relative to what you say matters most.

- How do your habits of sleeping, eating and exercising affect your available energy?
- How much negative energy do you invest in defense spending—frustration, anger, fear, resentment, envy—as opposed to positive energy utilized in the service of growth and productivity?
- How much energy do you invest in yourself, and how much in others, and how comfortable are you with that balance? How do those closest to you feel about the balance you've struck?
- How much energy do you spend worrying about, feeling frustrated by and trying to influence events beyond your control?
- Finally, how wisely and productively are you investing your energy?

To focus more specifically on how your energy management choices are affecting your performance, the chart that follows lists the most common performance barriers that we encounter with our clients. We call them barriers to full engagement because they impede the optimal flow of energy.

Whether it is impatience, or lack of empathy, or poor time management, they are problematic because they have negative energy consequences—in your own life and on others. As you look through this chart, think about the impact that each of these barriers has on the quality and quantity of energy in your work and in your personal life.

If you took our suggestion in the first chapter, you have already logged on to our web site, filled out the Full Engagement Inventory and gotten back your results. Ideally, you now also have the cumulative feedback from five people who know you well. Gathering this information can be painful but also immensely revealing—and ultimately very rewarding. The more data you have at your disposal, the better equipped you are to identify your top five performance barriers. When it comes to making specific changes in the way you manage your energy in the service of performance, these barriers will help guide your choices about what new, positive rituals to build in your life.

COMMON PERFORMANCE BARRIERS

Low energy	Lack of trust in others
Impatience	Lack of integrity
Defensiveness	Indecisive
Negative attitude	Poor communication skills
Critical of others	Poor listening skills

Low stress tolerance
Moody/irritable
Poor team player
Inflexible/rigid
Unfocused
High anxiety
Poor time management

Lack of passion
Low self-confidence
Lack of empathy
Overly dependent
Poor work-life balance
Negative/pessimistic thinking

PERCEPTION AND REALITY

Another way that we deceive ourselves is by assuming that our view represents the truth when it is really just an interpretation, a lens through which we choose to view the world. Without realizing it, we often create stories around a set of facts and then take our stories to be the truth. Just because something feels real to us doesn't make it so. The facts in a given situation may be incontrovertible, but the meaning that we ascribe to them is often far more subjective.

In the aftermath of a meeting that he had spent weeks trying to arrange, Toby B., a salesman for a computer company, left feeling very encouraged about the prospects for closing a major deal. The next day, he wrote his potential customer a follow-up email and suggested a second meeting. After several days, he had received no response. He wrote a second email and this time a week went by with no response. Toby decided to call, and he left his prospective customer a voice mail. Once again, no answer. Now Toby's story began to kick in, a variation on one that he had told himself many times before in the face of discouragement. "Obviously, this guy isn't interested after all," he concluded. "I was just kidding myself about how well the original meeting went, I must have screwed up in some way. I've had this happen a lot of times lately, and there is obviously something wrong with the way I'm selling." Feeling frustrated and slightly humiliated, he decided not to follow up again.

Two weeks went by and over dinner one night, Toby recounted his story to his friend Gail. She had a totally different interpretation of the same set of facts. "Isn't it true that you've made several big sales in the last six months?" she asked. "You have told me yourself that these are big-ticket items you're trying to sell and it never happens quickly. If this guy seemed enthusiastic after you left the meeting, I'm sure he really was. He probably just got really busy, and it dropped off his radar screen. Why don't you wait another week and write him an email as if you're following up for the first time?"

Reluctantly and skeptically, Toby took Gail's advice. Ten minutes after he sent the new email, he received a response from his prospective customer "Apologies," it began. "I forgot to mention that I was just leaving for a two-week vacation when we met. I'm still enthusiastic. Let's set up a meeting to take the next steps."

Toby had allowed himself to be defeated by the story he told himself rather than by the truth. His friend, fortunately, found a more motivating way to look at the same situation, which helped transform Toby's attitude and the quality of his energy. As the psychologist Martin Seligman puts it: "When our explanatory beliefs take the form of personal, permanent and pervasive factors (It's my fault . . . it's always going to be like this . . . it's going to affect everything I do"), we give up and become paralyzed. When our explanations take the opposite form, we become energized." In the absence of confirmation, neither Toby's nor Gail's interpretation was necessarily more truthful than the other, but a more optimistic take was clearly more empowering.

It is both a danger and a delusion when we become too identified with any singular view of ourselves—for better or for worse. We open to a more complete picture when we can step back and develop the capacity for self-observation. By broadening our perspective, we can become the audience for the drama in our lives rather than becoming identified with the drama itself. The practice of Vipassana meditation is sometimes referred to as "witnessing"—observing our thoughts, feelings and sensations without getting caught up in them. As the psychiatrist Robert Assagioli puts it, we may move from a feeling of "I am overwhelmed by my anxiety" to the more dispassionate "My anxiety is trying to overwhelm me." In one, we are victims. In the other, we have the power to make choices and take action.

"I COULD BE WRONG"

Julie D. is an executive coach who came through our program. Accustomed to dispensing advice for a living, she was very comfortable providing answers for people. The problem occurred on those infrequent occasions when a client strongly resisted something that she said. Her immediate instinct was to see the person as rigid, defensive and unwilling to look honestly at himself. With some probing, it became clear that Julie herself had a dread of being wrong, and a fierce aversion to feeling criticized. Although she wasn't aware of it, entertaining a point of view contrary to hers prompted a sense of powerlessness and felt like a threat to her self-esteem. The result was that Julie spent enormous energy defending her vision. Perceptive as she was, she lacked the capacity to see the world through any lens but her own.

The comedian Dennis Miller is known for his rants—monologues during which he hilariously eviscerates the famous and powerful, poking fun at their inflated sense of self-importance and their hypocrisy. He concludes each rant with a disarming line: "Of course that's just my opinion," he says. "I could be wrong." It is a charming, subtle way of sticking a pin in his own balloon, of acknowledging the possibility that he may be just as full of himself as the folks he is sending up. For Julie, the challenge was to relax her own defensiveness and rigidity, and to see the ways it was sometimes distorting her ability to see the truth about herself and her clients.

Facing the truth requires that we retain an ongoing openness to the possibility that we may not be seeing ourselves—or others—accurately. In a graphic example of the mutual entailment of the virtues, confidence unmediated by humility becomes grandiosity, egomania and even fanaticism. In his book *Good to Great*, Jim Collins and a team of researchers studied the qualities of CEOs whose companies had dramatically improved their performance during the previous years. To his surprise, Collins found that it was not the most charismatic or visibly brilliant leaders who built the most successful companies. Rather it was the leaders who demonstrated a balanced blend of two seemingly paradoxical qualities: fierce resolve and humility.

It is hardly surprising that the ability to persevere in the face of setbacks is critical to success. But why were the most successful leaders also so consistently self-effacing, modest and eager to share credit? In part, it was that their humility gave others room to flourish. They recognized instinctively that the success of any large venture depends on giving people a sense of ownership and a feeling of being valued and valuable. Genuine humility also meant that these leaders were open to opinions contrary to their own and to the possibility that their views weren't always necessarily right. They were confident enough to be wrong without feeling diminished as a result. When we aren't investing energy in protecting our turf, we have the potential to see more of the truth and to continue to learn and grow. In the course of building this model and change process, we have learned this lesson ourselves dozens of times. Passionate as we are about what we teach, we know that it is forever a work in progress. We do not have all the answers and our ideas will continue to evolve in the crucible of experience, inquiry and openness to other points of view.

"HOW IS THAT ME?"

Difficult and unpleasant as it may be to accept, we often feel most hostile to those who remind us of aspects of ourselves that we prefer not to see. "Ask someone to give a description of the personality type which he finds most despicable, most unbearable and hateful, and most impossible to get along with," writes Edward Whitmont, "and he will produce a description of his own repressed characteristics. . . . These very qualities are so unacceptable to him precisely because they represent his own repressed side; only that which we cannot accept within ourselves do we find impossible to live with in others." Think for a moment of someone you actively dislike. What quality in that person do you find most objectionable? Now ask yourself, "How am I that?"

Julie, the executive coach, reported a remarkable transformation when she began asking herself a variation on this question any time that someone disagreed with her and she felt certain that she was right: "How might the opposite of what I'm thinking or feeling also be true?" Once she could bring this possibility to light, recognizing that it might have validity without diminishing her, her defensiveness began to recede. In aikido, the warrior gains his advantage by blending with the aggression of his opponent rather than fighting against him directly. Until we embrace all of who we are, we remain our own worst enemies.

Psychologist James Hillman argues that we must ultimately find a balance between self-acceptance and an ongoing commitment to change those aspects of ourselves that are destructive:

> Loving oneself is no easy matter . . . because it means loving all of oneself, including the shadow where one is inferior and socially so unacceptable. The care one gives this humiliating part is the cure . . . [but] the moral dimension can never be abandoned. Thus is the cure a paradox requiring two incommensurables: the moral recognition that these parts of me are burdensome and intolerable and must change, and the loving laughing acceptance which takes them just as they are, joyfully,

forever. One both tries hard and lets go, both judges harshly and joins gladly . . .

If the truth is to set us free, facing it cannot be a one-time event. Rather, it must become a practice. Like all of our "muscles," self-awareness withers from disuse and deepens when we push past our resistance to see more of the truth. We fall asleep to aspects of ourselves each and every day. Much as we must keep returning to the gym and pushing weight against resistance in order to sustain or increase our physical strength, so we must persistently shed light on those aspects of ourselves that we prefer not to see in order to build our mental, emotional and spiritual capacity.

At the same time, it is not healthy to relentlessly seek the truth any more than it is to continuously stress our biceps. As the anthropologist Gregory Bateson put it: "There is always an optimal value beyond which anything is toxic, no matter what: oxygen, sleep, psychotherapy, philosophy." When it comes to absorbing the truth, too big a dose can be overwhelming, and even self-defeating. Some truths are too unbearable to be absorbed all at once. In the aftermath of the anthrax scare, for example, it made sense to know some facts about anthrax, including how to recognize its symptoms and how best to treat it. To dwell on the threat, however, was more likely to be paralyzing than it was productive, more energy draining rather than empowering.

The Serenity Prayer is a perfect primer on ideal energy management: "God grant me the serenity to accept the things I cannot change; the courage to change the things I can; and the wisdom to know the difference." We spend vast quantities of energy worrying about people and situations over which we have no control. Far better to concentrate our energy on that which we can influence. Facing the truth helps us to make the distinction.

To the degree that our sense of self-worth is fragile, opening to unpleasant information about ourselves can feel threatening. We need courage to jump into the unknown but also compassion for our resistance to accepting what we discover. We must keep moving deliberately in the direction of truth, recognizing that the forces of self-protection will slow our progress at times. As we clear our sight lines, we become more aware of the blocks that stand in our way. Facing the most difficult truths in our lives is challenging but also liberating. When we have nothing left to hide, we no longer fear exposure. Vast energy is freed up to fully engage in our lives. We celebrate our strengths and continue to build them. When we make a misstep, we take responsibility for it and reset our course.

BEAR IN MIND

- Facing the truth frees up energy and is the second stage, after defining purpose, in becoming more fully engaged.

254

- Avoiding the truth consumes great effort and energy.
- At the most basic level, we deceive ourselves in order to protect our self-esteem.
- Some truths are too unbearable to be absorbed all at once. Emotions such as grief are best metabolized in waves.
- Truth without compassion is cruelty—to others and to ourselves.
- What we fail to acknowledge about ourselves we often continue to act out unconsciously.
- A common form of self-deception is assuming that our view represents the truth, when it is really just a lens through which we choose to view the world.
- Facing the truth requires that we retain an ongoing openness to the possibility that we may not be seeing ourselves—or others—accurately.
- It is both a danger and a delusion when we become too identified with any singular view of ourselves. We are all a blend of light and shadow, virtues and vices.
- Accepting our limitations reduces our defensiveness and increases the amount of positive energy available to us.

CHAPTER 10

TAKING ACTION:
THE POWER OF POSITIVE
RITUALS

Ivan Lendl was far from the most physically gifted tennis player of his era, but for five years he was the number-one-ranked player in the world. His edge was in the routines that he built. It is no surprise that Lendl practiced long hours on the court, or even that he did so at very precise times. What set him apart from other players on the tour was that he followed similar routines in every dimension of his life. He developed a rigorous fitness regimen off the court, which included sprints, middle-distance runs, long bicycle rides and strength training. He did regular ballet bar exercises to increase his balance and grace. He adhered to a low-fat, high complex-carbohydrate diet and ate at very specific times.

Lendl also practiced a series of daily mental-focus exercises to improve his concentration—and regularly introduced new ones to assure that they remained challenging. At tournaments, he gave clear instructions to friends and family not to burden him with issues that might distract him from his mission. Whatever he did, he was either fully engaged or strategically disengaged. He even meticulously scheduled his time for relaxation and recovery, which included recreational golf, daily afternoon naps and regularly scheduled massages. On the court, during matches, he relied on another set of rituals to keep himself centered and focused, including visualizing entire points before playing them and following the same multiple-step ritual each time he stepped up to the line to serve. As longtime rival John McEnroe later said: "Much as I may have disliked him, I have to give Lendl credit. Nobody in the sport has ever worked as hard as he did. . . . Ivan wasn't the most talented player, but his dedication—physical and mental, was incredible, second to none . . . and he did it all through rehearsal."

Tiger Woods is the modern version of Lendl, albeit with considerably more talent, but with the same fierce dedication to rituals for managing energy in all dimensions of his life—physical, emotional, mental and spiritual. The payoff is clear. By his early twenties, Woods had become not only simply the best at what he does, but also the most consistently dominating golfer in the history of the game.

It is perfectly logical to assume that Lendl excelled in part because he had extraordinary will and discipline. That probably isn't so. A growing body of research suggests that as little as 5 percent of our behaviors are consciously self-directed. We are creatures of habit and as much as 95 percent of what we do occurs automatically or in reaction to a demand or an anxiety. What Lendl understood brilliantly and instinctively was the power of positive rituals—precise, consciously acquired behaviors that become automatic in our lives, fueled by a deep sense of purpose.

Positive energy rituals are powerful on three levels. They help us to insure that we effectively manage energy in the service of whatever mission we are on. They reduce the need to rely on our limited conscious will and discipline to take action. Finally, rituals are a powerful means by which to translate our values and priorities into action—to embody what matters most to us in our everyday behaviors.

EXPEDIENT ADAPTATION

Like so many of us, Roger B. had become a prisoner of his negative energy habits and routines. Many of these choices were expedient—strategies for quickly marshaling energy without regard to the long-term energy consequences. Skipping breakfast made it possible for Roger to get to the office earlier but took no account of the effect that this choice had on his energy capacity throughout the morning. Drinking caffeinated coffee and diet colas was Roger's way of artificially pumping up his energy in the face of inadequate sleep. Not exercising was a consequence of Roger's inability to push himself physically when he felt so drained by other demands. It was difficult for Roger to imagine that once he built some endurance, exercising might actually be a source of renewal—not just physically after long hours at his desk, but also mentally and emotionally.

Impatience and irritation were a means for Roger to vent his frustration—without regard for the toll that these negative emotions took on others and on his own energy reserves. Several drinks at night and the occasional cigarette were strategies Roger adopted to get immediate relief from stress—but they robbed him of energy in the short term and threatened his health in the long term. Keeping a certain distance from his wife and children was a means by which to avoid one more demand on his limited energy stores but at a cost to the emotional nourishment that comes from close relationships. Above all, Roger had adapted by disengaging—conserving energy by not investing too much of it in anything or allowing himself to think too deeply about the choices that he was making.

Roger's halfhearted attempts to change his behavior had been short-lived and ultimately unsuccessful. He was scarcely alone. Most of us are frustrated in our attempts to change, victims of the New Year's resolution syndrome in which we make firm commitments to new behaviors, only to quickly fall back into our familiar patterns. Rituals serve as anchors, insuring that even in the most difficult circumstances we will continue to use our energy in service of the values that we hold most dear. We are all exposed to storms throughout our lives—sickness and disease; the death of loved ones; betrayal and disappointments; financial setbacks and layoffs from jobs. These are the situations in which our character is truly tested and our choices about how to manage energy are critical.

**The bigger the storm,
the more inclined we are
to revert to our survival habits,
and the more important
positive rituals become.**

Great performers, whether they are athletes or fighter pilots, surgeons or Special Forces soldiers, FBI agents or CEOs, all rely on positive rituals to manage their energy and achieve their goals. The same is true, we have discovered, of anyone whose life is grounded in clearly defined values. "Every time we participate in a ritual, we are expressing our beliefs, either verbally or more implicitly," write Evan Imber-Black and Janine Roberts, authors of *Rituals for Our Times*. "Families who sit down to dinner together every night are saying without words that they believe in the need for families to have shared time together. . . . Nightly bedtime rituals offer parents and children an opportunity to tell each other what they believe about all kinds of matters. The sheer act of doing the bedtime ritual expresses a belief in a certain kind of parent–child relationship where warmth and affection and safety are available."

It is easy to dismiss as rigid and even extreme the highly structured routines of an athlete like Ivan Lendl. But stop for a moment and think about the people you admire—or simply look at the areas of your life in which you are most effective and productive. If you are like most of our clients, you already have many rituals in place—often outside your conscious awareness. These may range from habits of hygiene, to planning for the day ahead, to routines with your family. Far from precluding spontaneity, rituals provide a level of comfort, continuity and security that frees us to improvise and to take risks. Think of a great athlete producing a seemingly impossible shot under fierce pressure; a highly trained surgeon making a critical counterintuitive decision at a life-or-death moment during a delicate operation; or an executive breaking an impasse in a difficult, formal negotiation by suddenly coming up with a novel structure for a deal. Rituals provide a stable framework in which creative breakthroughs often occur. They can also open up time for recovery and renewal, when relationships can be deepened and spiritual reflection becomes possible.

The limitations of conscious will and discipline are rooted in the fact that every demand on our self-control—from deciding what we eat to managing frustration, from building an exercise regimen to persisting at a difficult task—all draw on the same small easily depleted reservoir of energy.

In a series of imaginative experiments, several

researchers have demonstrated how this plays out in everyday life. In one study, for example, subjects were deprived of food for several hours and then exposed to a plate of chocolate-chip cookies and other sweets. One group was given permission to indulge themselves. A second group was asked to refrain from eating sweets and to settle for radishes instead. The latter group succeeded in resisting the sweets, but then demonstrated significantly less persistence than the first group in a follow-up test trying to solve insoluble puzzles. In a second experiment, dieters who were presented with tempting food were able to control themselves but became significantly more likely to break the diet when faced with subsequent temptations. In still a third experiment, one group of subjects was asked to hold their hands under ice water for a specified period of time. They performed significantly worse on a series of subsequent proofreading tasks than a group that had not been subjected to the ice-water challenge.

The sustaining power of rituals comes from the fact that they conserve energy. "We should not cultivate the habit of thinking of what we are doing," wrote philosopher A. N. Whitehead, back in 1911. "The precise opposite is the case. Civilization advances by extending the number of operations which we can perform without thinking about them." In contrast to will and discipline, which imply pushing ourselves to action, a well-defined ritual pulls us. We feel somehow worse if we don't do it. Think about brushing your teeth or taking a shower or kissing your spouse goodbye in the morning or attending your child's soccer games or calling your parents on a weekend. If we want to build into our lives new behaviors that last, we can't spend much energy to sustain them.

Since will and discipline are far more limited and precious resources than most of us realize, they must be called upon very selectively. Because even small acts of self-control use up this limited reservoir, consciously using this energy for one activity means it will be less available for the next one. The sobering truth is that we have the capacity for very few conscious acts of self-control in a day.

Much as it is possible to strengthen a bicep or a tricep by subjecting it to stress and then recovering, so it is possible to strategically build the muscle of self-control. The same training regimen applies. Exercise self-control or empathy or patience past normal limits, and then allow time for rest and these muscles become progressively stronger. More reliably, however, we can offset the limitations of conscious will and discipline by building positive rituals that become automatic—and relatively effortless—as quickly as possible.

THE RITUALS OF STRESS AND RECOVERY

The most important role of rituals is to insure an effective balance between energy expenditure and energy renewal in the service of full engagement.

All great performers have rituals that optimize their ability to move rhythmically between stress and recovery. Jim's discovery of the between-point recovery rituals, used by nearly all top tennis players, is an especially vivid example. In just sixteen to twenty seconds, these highly precise rituals prompt a remarkably efficient form of recovery.

The same stress-recovery balance is critical in any venue that demands performance. The more precise and effective our recovery rituals, the more quickly we can restore our energy reserves. We have done a great deal of work with Wall Street traders, for example, who must sit in front of their computer terminals for long hours each day, and have very limited time for breaks. When we first suggested that they needed to build more recovery rituals into their days, they laughed at us.

"We barely have time to go to the bathroom," they told us. "How are we going to take time for recovery?" We reminded them how quickly and efficiently athletes are able to recover and pointed out that even structured sixty- to ninety-second breaks throughout the day could provide a great deal of renewal. With our encouragement, they began devising their own rituals. These ranged from sixty seconds of deep breathing to putting on a Walkman and listening to a favorite song; from making a quick call home to check in and connect with a spouse or a child to walking up and down four flights of stairs; from playing a video game on the computer screen to eating an energy bar. The more scheduled and systematic these rituals became, the more renewal they provided.

Peter D. is a writer who sought our advice at a time when he was facing a highly challenging book deadline that he wasn't sure he could meet. For years, Peter was used to putting in long continuous hours at his word processor. The problem, he told us, was that he found it hard to maintain his concentration, particularly as the day wore on. Our goal was to help him to shift from the mentality of a marathoner to that of a sprinter. We worked with Peter to develop rituals that alternated periods of intense engagement with relatively short but highly structured periods of recovery.

Because Peter told us that he felt freshest early in the morning, we had him begin his workdays at 6:30 a.m. and write for ninety minutes before he did anything else. To minimize distraction, he agreed to turn off his phone and not to check his email during his writing hours. At 8:00 a.m., Peter stopped to have breakfast with his wife and three children. We also suggested that he shift from his previous routine of eating a bagel or a muffin and a glass of orange juice, to the more sustaining energy of a protein drink. Peter returned to work at 8:30 a.m. and wrote without interruption until 10:00. At that point, he took a twenty-minute recovery break—ten minutes of training with light weights followed by ten minutes of meditation. He also ate a piece of fruit or a handful of nuts before heading back to his desk.

Peter's third writing session went from 10:30 until 12:00 noon, at which point he went jogging and then ate lunch. During those 41/2 hours of focused morning work, Peter was able to write nearly twice as much as had sitting at his desk for up to ten hours a day in previous years. In the afternoons, he turned his attention to reading and research for the book, and to other business. In the evenings, feeling good about his productivity but also reasonably rested, Peter still had the energy to focus on his family.

The more exacting the challenge, the more rigorous our rituals need to be. The preparation of soldiers for combat is a good example. The rituals of basic training are so exacting—especially in the Marines—that soft, fearful and slovenly teenagers can be transformed into lean, confident, mission-driven soldiers in just eight to twelve weeks. Recruits are compelled to build rituals in every dimension of their lives—how they walk and how they talk; what time they go to bed and wake up; when and what they eat; how they take care of their bodies and how they think and act under pressure. This code of conduct makes it possible for them to do the right thing at the right time even in the face of the most severe of all stresses—the threat of death.

CONTINUITY AND CHANGE

Rituals also help us to create structure in our lives. More than ever, we are bombarded by competing options and choices, endless information and infinite demands. As one top executive at a leading financial firm told us: "The biggest problem in American business today is the feeling that nothing is ever finished. There is no satisfaction to be derived from a job well done because there is always another demand to be met. We're all running on an endless treadmill." Rituals create boundaries—clearly delineated opportunities to renew and refuel but also to take stock and to prepare for the next challenge.

Each time Ivan Lendl stepped up to the line to serve during a tennis match, he predictably wiped his brow with his wristband, knocked the head of his racquet against each of his heels, took sawdust from his pocket, bounced the ball four times and visualized where he intended to hit the ball. In the process, Lendl was recalibrating his energy: pushing away distraction, calming his physiology, focusing his attention, triggering reengagement and preparing his body to perform at its best. In effect, he was programming his internal computer. When the point began, the program ran automatically. Successful executives, managers and salespeople often have their own pre-performance rituals. In advance of an important meeting, these rituals might range from taking a walk in order to shift gears to abdominal breathing in order to relax; from rehearsing the key points to be covered to reciting a series of affirmations around desired outcomes.

In addition to creating continuity, rituals help

to facilitate change. For thousands of years rituals have been used to take account of our accomplishments, give thanks for our blessings and facilitate the transition from one stage to another in our lives. We mark rites of passage with the bar mitzvah in Judaism, the confirmation in Christianity and with celebrations around birthdays, anniversaries and graduations. Holiday rituals such as Thanksgiving and Christmas provide opportunities to give thanks, to take stock and to reconnect with loved ones. Weddings mark the movement from single to married life—simultaneously celebrating the promise of the future while acknowledging the momentousness of the transition. More broadly, rituals imbue certain key events in our lives with meaning.

Unfortunately, many of us have negative associations with rituals. In part, this may be because rather than freely being chosen, they were imposed upon us early in our lives. When a ritual begins to feel empty, stale and even oppressive, the likely explanation is that it has lost its connection to deeply held values. To keep rituals alive and vibrant requires a delicate balance. Without the structure and clarity they provide, we are forever vulnerable to the urgent demands in our lives, the seductions of the moment and the limits of our conscious will and discipline. On the other hand, if our rituals become too rigid, unvarying and linear, the eventual consequence is boredom, disengagement and even diminished passion and productivity.

Our dual challenge is to hold fast to our rituals when the pressures in our lives threaten to throw us off track, and to periodically revisit and change them so that they remain fresh. It is critical, for example, to create structured workouts as part of any weight-training regime. However, if you continue to challenge the same body parts in the same way, you will eventually stop gaining strength, become bored and frustrated, and likely quit. Healthy rituals straddle the territory between the comfort of the past and the challenge of the future. Used to best advantage, rituals provide a source of security and consistency without thwarting change or undermining flexibility.

KEY BEHAVIORS

There are several key elements in building effective energy-management rituals but none so important as specificity of timing and the precision of behavior during the thirty- to sixty-day acquisition period. Ted D. and his wife, Donna, went through our program together. Like many of our clients, they complained that because their lives were so busy, they had too little time for one another. As it happened, they also worked together, running a mail-order catalog business. Most of their conversations, on and off the job, focused either on business or on dealing with the demands of their three teenage children.

Ted and Donna decided to build a ritual around

269

setting aside an hour and a half of uninterrupted time for one another on Saturday mornings. The first time that the designated day arrived, both of them had a couple of other pressing items to take care of first. By the time they were ready to talk, an hour had passed. Just as they were about to start, one of their kids awakened and wanted a ride to an athletic event. Before they knew it, the pressing nature of the day overcame their commitment to spend time together.

When much the same thing happened the second week, Ted suggested that they set a specific start time—8:00 a.m.—and make it sacrosanct. They agreed not to answer the phone during their time together, and they asked their kids not to interrupt them. It worked immediately. Within a few weeks, however, a second issue emerged. Because Ted was more aggressive in talking about what was on his mind, he tended to take up the majority of their time together. To solve the problem, they agreed that Donna should go first, and that for the first forty-five minutes they would talk about whatever was on her mind. Then they switched roles and Ted took his turn. When we last spoke to them, it had been more than two years since they launched the ritual, and they had missed it perhaps half a dozen times. It had become deeply woven into the fabric of their lives, and both of them agreed that it had been a central factor in helping them to feel closely connected no matter how busy the rest of their lives become.

Doug L. is an executive who spent nearly a decade overseeing several thousand financial advisers at a large financial services company. From early on, he instinctively understood the role of rituals. To assure that he embodied the values he had defined as important and the goals he had set for himself, he developed a series of what he called "key behaviors." In his personal life these included a weekly date night with his wife and a commitment to attend all of his daughters' athletic events. One of the more unusual rituals, for an executive at his level, was that on Wednesdays at 1:00 p.m., he left his office to play tennis for an hour, and on Fridays at 1:00 p.m. he played basketball for ninety minutes at a nearby YMCA. His secretary put these two dates in his weekly calendar and protected them the way she would any other high-priority appointment. For Doug, these two activities were critical sources of renewal in the course of his very demanding days. If he had been more casual about trying to find the time to exercise in the middle of workdays, he told us, it never would have happened. The same was true of the date night with his wife and the time he committed to his daughters.

PRECISION AND SPECIFICITY

A broad and persuasive array of studies confirms that specificity of timing and precision of behavior dramatically increase the likelihood of success. The explanation lies once again in the fact that our conscious capacity for self-control is limited and easily depleted. By determining when, where and how a behavior will occur, we no longer have to think much about getting it done. A series of experiments have confirmed this pattern. In one study, for example, participants were asked to write a report on how they intended to spend Christmas Eve, and to submit it within forty-eight hours. Half of the participants were told to specify exactly when and where they intended to write the report. The other half got no such deadline. Among those who had the precise deadline, 75 percent handed the reports in on time. Only one-third of the second group did so.

In another study, women were asked to perform a breast self-examination during the subsequent month. One group was asked to write down when and where they would do so, while the other was not. Both groups were then narrowed down to those women who had expressed a strong intention to complete the task. Nearly 100 percent of those who designated when and where they would do the exam completed it. Only 53 percent of the second group did so, despite equally strong intentions to conduct the exam.

In still a third study, the goal was to increase compliance in an fitness program that was being offered to a group of nonexercising college students. In a first attempt to motivate them, the subjects were given data about how exercise would significantly reduce their vulnerability to coronary heart disease. Participation in the program increased from 29 to 39 percent. When this information was followed by a request that students designate when and where they intended to exercise, compliance went to a remarkable 91 percent. Similar results were achieved in trying to help people adopt better eating habits. Participants proved far more likely to eat healthy, low calorie foods when they were asked in advance to specify precisely what they intended to eat for each of their meals during the day, rather than using their energy to resist eating certain foods all day long.

In perhaps the most dramatic experiment of all, a group of drug addicts were studied during withdrawal—a time when the energy required to control the urge to take drugs severely compromises their ability to undertake nearly any other task. As part of the effort to help them find employment post-rehabilitation, one group was asked to commit to writing a short résumé before 5:00 p.m. on a particular day. Not a single one succeeded. A second group was asked to complete the same task, but also to say exactly when and where they would write the résumé. Eighty percent of that group succeeded.

The specificity and precision of rituals also makes it more likely that we will be able to produce them under pressure. Bill Walsh, the brilliant former coach of the San Francisco 49ers, put it simply in describing his approach to football: "At all times the focus must be on doing things properly. Every play. Every practice. Every meeting. Every situation.

Every time." Walsh's point applies to any performance venue. Practice makes perfect only if the practice is perfect—or at least aims for perfection. If you cannot perform a particular task effectively when you are feeling relaxed and unpressured, it is unlikely that you will be able to do so when the pressure is high, or when you are in the midst of a crisis. Building precise rituals makes it possible to push away the distractions and fears that arise under pressure. "The less thinking people have to do under adverse circumstances, the better," explains Walsh. "When you're under pressure, the mind can play tricks on you. The more primed and focused you remain, the smoother you can deal with out-of-the-ordinary circumstances."

Precision and specificity also help to assure that our rituals themselves remain fueled by our deepest values. It is not enough simply to create a vision statement. Only by building a ritual to regularly revisit this vision can we insure a strong, continuing connection to the unique source of energy such a statement provides. Pediatric neurosurgeon Ben Carson is a good example. "I have found that having a morning ritual—meditation or some quiet reading time—can set the tone for the whole day," he explains. "Every morning, I spend a half hour reading the Bible, especially the Book of Proverbs. There's so much wisdom there. During the day, if I encounter a frustrating situation. I think back to one of the verses that I read that morning. Take Proverbs 16:32, for example: 'He who is slow to anger is better than the mighty and he who rules his spirit is better than he who takes a city.' "

Our clients have found their own rituals to maintain their connection to the energy of purpose. Some spend a few minutes when they wake up writing in a journal. Others meditate or pray or read something inspirational or simply spend a few minutes in reflection while they are showering. Still others have their vision statements on the home page of their computers, or make it a practice during breaks to reflect on their values. One client had his personal and professional vision laminated on two sides of an index card and slipped it under the visor above his seat in his car. On his way to work in the morning, he spent a few minutes reviewing his professional vision. On his way home at night, he flipped the card and spent the last few minutes of his commute reflecting on his personal vision. The key is not how we make the connection to our purpose. Rather it is assuring that we do so in a regular way.

DOING VS. NOT DOING

When intentions are framed negatively—"I won't overeat" or "I will not get angry"—they rapidly deplete our limited stores of will and discipline. Not doing something requires continuous self-control. This is especially true of deeply ingrained habits and responses to temptations, such as eating desserts or drinking alcohol in a social situation. Designing a positive behavior to prepare for a particular situation is sometimes called "priming." In the case of the temptation to overeat, for example, the priming ritual might be something like "When I am tempted by dessert, I will have a piece of fruit instead."

For years, George F., an executive at a small consulting company, struggled with an inclination to lose his temper whenever he felt frustrated or thwarted. It undermined his relationships at work, and because he considered kindness a primary value, it also made him feel bad about himself. As we looked more closely, it became clear that George was especially vulnerable to blowing up when he had worked long hours without a break, or failed to eat at regular intervals. Countless times he had committed to controlling his impulses, but within a few days, he always found himself reverting to his familiar pattern.

Ensuring breaks and eating regularly represented a first intervention. Next, we suggested that George focus on the behavior he wanted to introduce into his life, rather than the one he hoped to resist. The first step was to get him to take several deep breaths as soon as he felt his anger rising and to resist saying anything in the moment. When he finally did speak, we suggested that George lower his voice. He had a tendency to speak louder as he became more aroused, which not only fueled his anger, but also pushed others away. Finally, we asked George to smile, even if it required a bit of acting at first. Considerable evidence suggests that smiling literally reduces arousal and short-circuits the "fight-or-flight" response. It is nearly impossible to smile and to feel angry at the same time.

Not surprisingly, George found this sequence of behaviors awkward and difficult at first. In several challenging situations, he simply forgot to do them at all. Within several weeks, however, the sequenced ritual had become nearly automatic in all but the most stressful circumstances. What George found most startling was that smiling in the face of frustration actually became a trigger to view the situation differently—more gently, less urgently and with a sense of humor.

INCREMENTAL CHANGE

If nothing succeeds like success, it is equally true that nothing fails like excess. Because change requires moving beyond our comfort zone, it is best initiated in small and manageable increments. Imagine that you decide, perhaps as a New Year's resolution, to finally get in shape and start paying more attention to your physical health. Flush with resolve and enthusiasm, you join a gym and make a commitment to jog and to work out with weights three times a week. In the same spirit, you vow to begin a diet, reducing your caloric intake by half and cutting out all sugars and simple carbohydrates. Finally, you commit to getting more sleep at night and to waking up an hour earlier each morning. You even make very specific and precise plans about how to initiate your new program.

Within ten days, your diet has failed, you've only gotten to the gym twice and you haven't changed your sleeping habits at all. What happened? The answer is that you took on too much, too quickly. Overwhelmed by the demands on your limited will and discipline, you rapidly depleted your self-regulatory reservoir. The result is not just that you failed to stick to your plan, but that you also likely fed your belief that it is impossible to change life-long habits.

Our method is to build rituals in increments—focusing on one significant change at a time, and setting reachable goals at each step of the process. If you have been completely sedentary and want to begin exercising, it doesn't make sense to start by trying to jog three miles a day five days a week. Your odds of success are far higher if you begin with a highly specific but carefully calibrated training plan. That might mean walking for fifteen minutes a day three times a week at first, with predetermined increases in time or pace built in for each subsequent week. Growth and change won't occur unless you push past your comfort zone, but pushing too hard increases the likelihood that you will give up. Far better to experience success at each step of a progressive process. Building confidence fuels the persistence to pursue more challenging changes. We call these "serial rituals."

BASIC TRAINING

In the Resources section, you will find a full Corporate Athlete Personal Development Plan, which will take you step-by-step through the process for identifying your key values, developing a vision, creating rituals that address your primary performance barriers and holding yourself accountable each day to your commitments. Two behaviors, we have found, dramatically increase the likelihood of successfully locking in new rituals during the typical thirty- to sixty-day acquisition period. We call these behaviors Basic Training. They serve as the ground upon which successful rituals are most effectively built.

Chart the Course   This practice can take many forms, but the aim is always the same: to launch each day's ritual-acquisition mission by revisiting our vision, clarifying not just what we intend to accomplish, but how we want to conduct ourselves along the way. Some of our clients find that they can do this in as little as five or ten minutes while others set aside a half hour or more. Some clients chart the course in the shower, while others sit in a quiet room at home or do it during a walk or a jog outdoors or even while commuting to work.

Charting the course may include different elements. Some clients find it most effective to connect to specific deeply held values such as generosity, empathy, honesty or confidence and to use them as fuel for instituting a particular behavior or achieving a specific goal. Others find it most powerful to actively imagine how they will handle potentially difficult challenges in the day ahead. Still others simply like to set aside a designated block of time when they get up to reflect on their vision for themselves. This may take the form of writing in a journal or meditation or prayer.

Sally F. worked at an inner-city public school. For all the idealism that drew her to teaching, she spent much of her day disciplining her students and trying to keep order in her classroom. She decided to institute a morning ritual to stimulate positive feelings about her work in order to offset frustration and increase her positive energy. After completing our training, she began launching each day by reconnecting with the importance of her four primary values: patience, respect for others, gratitude and humility.

On stressful days, it had always been difficult for Sally to resist succumbing to negative emotions. Living by a code of conduct about how to manage her energy—establishing rules of engagement—grounded Sally in her deepest values and helped her to keep discouragement at bay. When her energy flowed more from a positive sense of appreciation for the opportunity that teaching provided, Sally not only felt more patient and balanced but also found that she had a more uplifting and inspiring impact on her students.

Chart the Progress   The second key to building

rituals that lead to sustaining change is holding yourself accountable at the end of each day. Accountability is a means of regularly facing the truth about the gap between your intention and your actual behavior. If you are trying to eat a healthier diet, it is critical to have rituals that define what and when you are going to eat, but also to measure at the end of each day how well you've followed your plan. If you have built a ritual around treating others with more respect, it is important to keep track of how effectively you are meeting that goal. The same is true for any endeavor to which you have committed yourself. Defining a desired outcome and holding yourself accountable each day gives focus and direction to the rituals that you build. For many of our clients, the best way to do this is to create a daily accountability log. This exercise can be as simple as a yes or no check on a sheet kept by the side of your bed. (See Resources for a sample Accountability Log.)

"It's great to know how to recharge your batteries, but it's even more important that you actually do it," Vinod Khosla, a partner at the venture capital firm Kleiner, Perkins, Caulfield and Byers told *Fast Company*. "I track how many times I get home in time to have dinner with my family. My assistant reports the exact number to me each month. Your company measures its priorities. People also need to place metrics around their priorities. . . . My goal is to be home for dinner twenty-five nights a month. Having a target number is key. . . . Keeping track of your behavior each month means that you don't slip up, because you know immediately whether your schedule is matching up with your priorities."

Holding your own feet to the fire doesn't require judging or punishing yourself when you fall short. Negative motivation, as we have seen, is short-lived and energy draining. At its best, accountability is both a protection against our infinite capacity for self-deception and a source of information about what still stands in our way. If you are falling short in implementing a particular ritual or achieving the outcome that you are seeking, several explanations are possible. It may be that the ritual isn't grounded in a value or a vision that is truly compelling to you. It may be the goal that you set is simply too ambitious and needs to be implemented more slowly and progressively. It could also be that the ritual you put in place is faulty and needs to be restructured. Often, the failure to follow through on a new ritual masks the benefit that you derive from holding on to an existing behavior and an unacknowledged resistance to changing it. Whatever the explanation, measuring your progress at the end of the day should be used not as a weapon against yourself, but as an instructive part of the change process. We can derive as much value from studying and understanding our failures as we can from celebrating and reinforcing our successes.

- Rituals serve as tools through which we effectively manage energy in the service of whatever mission we are on.
- Rituals create a means by which to translate our values and priorities into action in all dimensions of our life.
- All great performers rely on positive rituals to manage their energy and regulate their behavior.
- The limitations of conscious will and discipline are rooted in the fact that every demand on our self-control draws on the same limited resource.
- We can offset our limited will and discipline by building rituals that become automatic as quickly as possible, fueled by our deepest values.
- The most important role of rituals is to insure effective balance between energy expenditure and energy renewal in the service of full engagement.
- The more exacting the challenge and the greater the pressure, the more rigorous our rituals need to be.
- Precision and specificity are critical dimensions of building rituals during the thirty- to sixty-day acquisition period.
- Trying not to do something rapidly depletes our limited stores of will and discipline.
- To make lasting change, we must build serial rituals, focusing on one significant change at a time.

CHAPTER 11

THE REENGAGED
LIFE OF ROGER B.

Roger B. was an unusually challenging client. It wasn't that his performance barriers were significantly more daunting than those we typically face. Rather his initial motivation to change was so low.

Not surprisingly, Roger arrived at our center with a chip on his shoulder. His boss had done his best to frame his visit to us as an opportunity, but Roger couldn't help but feel that he had been singled out. He was late getting his pre-training materials to us, he wore his skepticism openly through much of the first day and he spent every break in our parking lot on his cell phone or answering emails on his BlackBerry. It was not an auspicious start.

As Roger moved through our Face the Truth process, he was clearly unsettled by what he was hearing. We consider that a hopeful sign. Until clients feel some discomfort about their current circumstances, they are rarely inclined to change. The first surprise for Roger was his physical testing results. He had continued to think of himself as being in relatively decent shape, but he was relying mostly on past memories. It hadn't occurred to him how much atrophy occurs over two decades of relative inactivity. He was discouraged to find how high his body fat percentage was and how low his cardiovascular capacity and strength were. He was also shocked when we told him that his risk factors—elevated blood pressure, relatively high alcohol consumption, chronic high stress, moderate smoking, high cholesterol and excess weight—made him a prime candidate for an early heart attack. It was true, he acknowledged, that his doctor had encouraged him to lose weight and to exercise more regularly, but Roger had never sensed that there was any urgency.

He was also surprised and a bit defensive about some of the feedback that he received from colleagues on his Full Engagement Inventory—most notably that they found him to be highly critical, impatient and short-tempered. While Roger admitted that he felt irritable and negative at times, he believed that he hid it well and that he generally treated others with respect and kindness. "These are tough times," he explained. "I think a lot of my people just aren't used to being under the kind of pressures we're facing, and they're blaming the messenger."

Roger's first real breakthrough occurred when we asked him whether his wife or children would describe him as impatient and irritable. He seemed to visibly shrink in his chair. Just a few weeks earlier, he told us, there had been an incident with Alyssa, his nine-year-old daughter. After picking her up at a Saturday gymnastics class, he had taken her out for lunch at a local restaurant— a rare occasion for the two of them to have time together alone. Alyssa was wearing a handknit sweater that Roger's mother had recently given her as a present. In the middle of lunch, Alyssa accidentally knocked over a glass of tomato juice and it got all over her new sweater.

Roger reacted angrily, chastising his daughter for her carelessness. Alyssa tried to apologize but Roger only became more angry. Eventually she began to sob. "All you ever do is yell at me," she said between tears. "Why do you hate me so much?" It was as if she had put a knife to his heart, Roger told us. Instantly, he realized that he had overreacted, taking out on Alyssa all the frustration and anxiety he was feeling at work. Worse yet, he realized that his daughter was right about his behavior. In the relatively little time that they spent together, he was often critical and impatient with her. The more he talked about it, the more he realized that the same was true with his younger daughter and with his wife as well. Perhaps, he told us, his colleagues were onto something about his behavior.

PURPOSE AS A FUEL

For the work of defining purpose, Roger's first evening homework assignment was to answer a series of questions designed to help him surface his most deeply held values. As we noted earlier, one of the questions we ask is: "Jump ahead to the end of your life: What are the three most important lessons you have learned?" Difficult as his life had become, Roger was not an especially complicated man. These were his answers:

1. Marry someone you love and respect and always make your family your highest priority. Everything else comes and goes, but your closest relationships are forever.
2. Work hard, keep your standards high, and never settle for anything less than you are capable of achieving.
3. Treat other people with respect and kindness.

The disparity between the story that Roger had told us the previous day and the lessons that he hoped to impart to his children didn't escape his notice. "I know I probably sound like a hypocrite," he said, "but even if I fall short, these really are the lessons I want to pass along to my kids." To the second query, "Think of someone you deeply respect. Describe the qualities you admire in this person," Roger chose his father, who it turned out had been a tailor and had later owned a dry cleaning business.

"I always admired his dignity and his gentleness and his integrity," Roger said. "He took great pride in his work, and he treated every one of his customers with interest and respect. He was the same way in our family. He never seemed to get frustrated or upset, even though he worked very long hours." As to who he was at his best, Roger described himself as "fun-loving, caring, dedicated, creative and totally reliable."

When it came to selecting his top five values, they weren't entirely surprising: kindness, excellence, family, integrity and health. "I think the first four were all strongly influenced by my parents," Roger told us. "In all honesty, I probably wouldn't have put health on my list before doing this program. But now that I see how much I've put myself at risk and what the consequences could be, health seems a lot more important than it did before.

The final step in defining purpose is to write a vision statement. This was Roger's:

My highest priority in life is my wife and my children. When we are together, I am committed to giving them all of my energy and attention. To make that possible, I must also take care of myself physically. At work, I hold myself to a high standard of excellence. As a leader I model each of my primary values—most of all kindness, concern for others and integrity. I make others feel cared for and confident that they can count on me. Whatever I do, I do wholeheartedly.

When it came time to build an action plan, Roger focused both on his primary values and on the performance barriers he had identified: low energy, impatience, negativity, lack of depth in relationships and lack of passion. He was reluctant to take on too much for fear of failing. We agreed. As we have pointed out, it is far better to succeed with small incremental changes and modest setbacks than to create a grand plan and fail completely. Roger decided to build his first set of rituals around increasing his physical capacity, not just to improve his health, but also on the theory that insufficient energy was a factor in every one of his performance issues.

The first ritual Roger created was to work out at least three times a week—Tuesdays and Fridays at 1:00 p.m. and Saturday mornings at 10:00 a.m. He also committed to a healthy, high-protein breakfast every day and to eating smaller, more nutritious meals at regular intervals throughout the day. The second area in which he hoped to build a ritual was spending more time with his family. The best he could come up with by the time he finished our training was to try to leave work no later than 6:30 p.m. each day and to limit dinners with clients to no more than two a week. He wanted to talk with his wife before devising more specific plans. Just making these changes, Roger believed, would have a significant impact on his energy, his relationships and his attitude at work. After two and a half days with us, he left feeling excited and enthusiastic about the challenge ahead.

HEADING HOME

Just before getting on the plane home from his training, Roger checked in to see what awaited him at work. He had 134 emails, forty-five voice mails and a half dozen small work crises that demanded his attention. To his dismay, he barely had time to say hello to his wife and children on the evening that he returned. After a quick hello, he disappeared into his home office and turned his attention to putting out fires at work. The next morning, he got up an hour earlier than usual and left before his family awoke, skipping his planned breakfast. Instead he gobbled down a donut and coffee from the deli next to his office. Roger spent the next four hours juggling a dozen issues and trying to catch up on calls and correspondence. For lunch, he grabbed the most convenient item— two slices of pizza from the cafeteria, which he ate at his desk. His first scheduled midday workout went by the wayside, and he rescheduled it in his mind for the next day. He had promised Rachel that he would try to get home early after three nights away, but by the time he forced himself to leave work, it was already 7:30 p.m.

On his commute home, feeling exhausted and discouraged, Roger began to brood. There was no way out, he decided. For all his optimistic plans, he was right back where he started. He wasn't going to arrive home before 8:30 p.m., he was certain that Rachel would be angry with him and he wasn't going to have much time or energy for his kids. A pile of work in his briefcase still demanded his attention.

When he got off the Interstate at his exit, Roger felt a surge of emotion that he couldn't fully understand. As he passed a local park five blocks from his house, the feelings inside him became so overwhelming that he couldn't continue driving. To his astonishment, the moment he pulled his car over, tears began to stream down his face. The last time he remembered crying was at his wedding twelve years earlier, and those had been tears of joy. These tears, he realized, were a reflection of some deep sadness about his life, and he had been holding them in for a long time. It occurred to Roger that what he really wanted to do was to go home and hug his wife and children and tell them how much he loved them and missed them.

Roger drove the last several blocks home feeling lighter and more buoyant. As he opened the front door, he called out for his children and his wife, but no one answered. He looked in the kitchen and the playroom to no avail. Rachel had long ago taught the children to give their father a wide berth on the nights that he arrived home late, knowing he would likely be feeling exhausted and irritable. On this occasion, however, Roger bounded up the stairs and found his girls playing together in Alyssa's room. The moment he saw them, he knelt down, held out his arms and they came running to him. He scooped them up and the tears began to stream down his face again. Moments later, Rachel walked in. She stopped in the doorway and a horrified look crossed her face.

"Oh my God," she said, "don't tell me. You've been fired."

Roger smiled through his tears. "No," he said, "it isn't that. I'm just so happy to see everyone."

The next morning Roger woke up feeling better than he had in years. He had breakfast with Rachel before the children got up. His morning at work was intense, but he forced himself to stick with his plan to exercise during his lunch hour at the health club near his office. It was the first time he had used the membership since a week after Rachel gave it to him for Christmas eight months earlier. When he finished his workout, Roger was physically tired but emotionally exhilarated. Instead of opting for a hamburger and fries at a fast-food restaurant near his office, he stopped at the local gourmet deli and made himself a light lunch from the salad bar. During the afternoon, he was less fatigued than he could remember feeling in a long time. At 6:30 sharp, he left for home.

As Roger approached the park near his house, he felt the same surge of emotion that he had the previous evening, and for a second time, he was compelled to pull over. To his utter amazement, his eyes again filled with tears, and the same intense desire to be with his family arose. This time when he walked into his house, he found his two daughters in the playroom. He held out his arms as they came running to him and once again he began to weep.

"Mommy," Alyssa yelled, "Daddy's crying again."

THE TRANSFORMATION

During the next six months, Roger was able to count on one hand the number of times that he returned home from work and failed to stop his car for at least a few minutes at the park near his house. The tears subsided, but the predictable surge of emotion did not. Stopping at the park became a ritual that permitted Roger to make a profound transition. Each time he parked his car, he left his work behind and took time to reconnect with why his family mattered so much to him and who he wanted to be when he was with them. For years, returning home at the end of the workday had felt like stepping from one set of exhausting demands into another. Now he began to experience his family as a powerful source of renewal. He became impeccable about his commitment to leave work by 6:30 p.m. and about his workouts.

Three weeks after returning home, Roger instituted a second ritual around his children. Because he left each morning before they awoke, he decided to write each of them a note each day and slip it under their doors. It was a way to connect with his daughters, even though he didn't see actually them, and to affirm their importance in his life. It also became a source of pleasure on its own terms. Some days, he wrote what he called "Roger's Rules of Order," usually in the form of short fables that he made up. On Sunday nights, he drew each of them a cartoon strip—something he had done for his college newspaper, but never since. When he was traveling, he sent an email to both girls in the mornings. Roger realized how important these rituals had become to his daughters one morning when he was rushed and failed to push a note under their doors. When he returned home that evening, both girls were waiting for him at the door with their arms folded. "Daddy, you forgot something this morning," Alyssa said.

Roger also instituted a morning ritual of eating breakfast with his wife—alternating oatmeal, egg-white omelets and a protein drink. Eating at home also gave him an opportunity to spend time with Rachel before the kids got up. The chance to connect for a few minutes of uninterrupted time each morning very quickly became precious to both of them. It was far more enriching than sitting in silence behind a morning newspaper. Instead, he spent three minutes skimming the headlines and saved a more careful reading for the evening after his kids were in bed. Within a couple of weeks, Roger felt a dramatic upturn in the quality and the quantity of his energy, both at home and at work.

Over the next couple of months, Roger launched two other rituals. The first was devoting the final fifteen minutes of his morning commute to thinking through the day ahead and revisiting his primary values. The second was making a call during his commute home to someone he cared about—his father and mother, one of his two siblings, or a friend. He could tell that his parents deeply appreciated hearing from him more often. The routine also became a great way to rekindle his connection with a good friend who had lived next door but had moved away the previous year. It turned out that the friend commuted home most nights at the same time that Roger did, and they began speaking for fifteen or twenty minutes, cell phone to cell phone, at least once a week.

Roger was also successful in sticking to his workout regimen. Within a month, he expanded it from three days to four, adding Sunday afternoons. Initially, he had planned just one workout on the weekends. He offered to take responsibility for the kids on the other day so that Rachel could have a couple of hours to work out herself. She was reluctant to be away from the children more than she already was during the week. Roger argued that she needed some time for herself and that working out would give her more positive energy when she was with them. Rachel finally suggested a compromise. It turned out that the local YMCA provided child care for parents using the facility, and so they joined as a family. Roger and Rachel began working out together on Saturday afternoons, and they brought their kids along. On Sunday at midday, Rachel went to work out by herself, while Roger took the girls out for brunch.

These rituals around working out, eating better and spending more focused time with his family were the primary ones that Roger undertook during the two months after he visited with us. While none of them related directly to his job, the changes he made not only influenced how he felt physically and his relationship with his family but also affected his productivity at the office. Feeling more positive and more energized, Roger became less edgy at work and he was able to concentrate better, especially in the afternoons after his work-outs. Because he was getting more done in less time, he felt comfortable about leaving work earlier. At least twice a week he was out the door by 5:30 p.m. and home by 6:30—a full hour earlier than at any point since he started his job a decade earlier. Eight weeks after he left us, we got a call from Roger's boss. "I don't know how you did it, but the guy is reborn," he told us. "It's like he's ten years younger and all fired up again."

GOING DEEPER

At three months, Roger began instituting several more rituals that were part of the second phase of his initial Action Plan. (See full plan in the Resources section that follows this chapter.) One was to better prioritize his work. Before coming to us, Roger had typically spent the first hour at the office answering emails and calls. Now, like many of our clients he committed himself to a routine of putting off responding to email and voice mail each morning until he first addressed at least one important, longer-range challenge.

His second ritual focused on being more rigorous about his breaks. While he had become meticulous about stopping at precisely 1:00 p.m. on the two days that he exercised, he still tended to work continuously for as much as three to four hours at a stretch. Roger decided to build in one recovery break in the morning and one in the afternoon. Browsing in bookstores was one of his favorite activities, and he began using his morning break to walk to the Barnes & Noble three blocks from his office and spending fifteen minutes there. In the afternoons, he used his break to check in with his girls as they returned home from school and then to do ten minutes of deep breathing at his desk. He also shifted his afternoon snack from a candy bar to half of an energy bar, a piece of fruit or a handful of nuts.

The third ritual that Roger launched was to have

a lunch with one of his direct reports every week—an outgrowth both of having defined kindness and respect for others as a primary value and a response to the feedback that he was critical and impatient. On the occasions that he felt it was important to give some kind of critical feedback, he made it a practice to begin and end by saying something positive.

At six months, Roger returned to our facility for a follow-up. From the moment that he walked in the door, it was clear that he had changed in significant ways. He looked healthier but also more animated, engaged and upbeat. The physical changes were immediately measurable. Roger had lost twelve pounds. His body-fat percentage had declined from 27 to 19 percent. His cholesterol level had dropped from 245 to 185 and his blood pressure was well within the normal range. When we tested him, his endurance had increased by almost 25 percent and his strength by 35 percent. We also asked Roger to rate his level of engagement. Where he had put it at 5 at work and a 3 at home six months earlier, he now put it at 9 for both.

BUMPS IN THE ROAD

Not every aspect of Roger's life was transformed. He admitted that he continued to smoke, especially on difficult days. He still wasn't satisfied with his level of integrity and responsibility—following through in a timely way on his commitments. Too

298

often, Roger told us, he continued to let sudden demands divert his attention from more important but less pressing priorities. When the demands mounted high enough, he still had a tendency to get impatient and curt with others. Roger told us that he was determined to create a ritual around behaving with more grace under pressure—using such situations not as an excuse for bad behavior but as a challenge to demonstrate leadership.

The other continuing struggle for Roger was maintaining his rituals when he traveled. As rigorous as he had become about them at home, he had yet to create comparable ones on the road. He rarely built in time to work out. He packed his schedule so tightly that he found it very difficult to take breaks. He was also less careful about his eating, skipping meals during the day and grabbing anything he could find between meetings. At dinner with clients, he still sometimes ate and drank too much.

We helped Roger to design one important new ritual and to extend several of his existing ones to his time on the road. The new ritual was aimed at helping him to deal better with high pressure—and to communicate more positive energy. We asked Roger to describe how he actually experienced pressure. What he felt first, he told us, was a rising anxiety in his chest, a flood of critical thoughts and a strong desire to seize control of the situation. When he found himself in those situations, we suggested that Roger begin by taking several deep abdominal breaths. We also asked him to think for a moment about someone whose method of handling tough situations he admired. He chose his boss. Finally, we asked him to visualize behaving the way that he imagined his boss would in crisis—and to use that as a model.

As for traveling, Roger realized that it was simply a matter of turning his attention to building rituals comparable to those he had at home. When it came to eating better, he decided that the most important ritual was to begin carrying healthy snacks with him so that he wouldn't be tempted to grab junk food on the run. The best time to work out on the road, he concluded, was before client dinners, which was also a way to decompress after a long day. Roger began scheduling his workout time the same way that he would any other meetings and not letting anything interfere. He also made sure that he was booked only in hotels with fitness centers. Finally, Roger committed to having no more than one glass of wine during dinners with clients and to sip at it very slowly.

There were times during the next several months, Roger reported, when a client ordered a particularly great bottle of wine, and the seductions were too great to resist. The same was true when it came to eating at a great restaurant. He also occasionally missed workouts when his schedule got too crowded. For the most part, however, Roger was successful at instituting his new travel rituals, even as he took some ribbing for fishing protein bars out of his briefcase in the middle of long meetings. After nine months, he reported that he had dropped an additional seven pounds.

No change proved more challenging for Roger—nor ultimately more satisfying—than learning to respond more gracefully under pressure. When he took the time to step back and walk himself through the ritual we had devised with him, Roger found that he was able to significantly reduce his reactivity. There were still occasions when the feeling of pressure to take action overwhelmed his capacity to be more reflective. With that in mind, he eventually created a second ritual for what he called "emergencies." In those situations, his tactic was simply to quietly nod his head in acknowledgment, regardless of what he was feeling, and then to say something like "I understand, and I'd like to take a little time to digest this before I respond." His primary commitment was not to react when he was feeling agitated or impatient. The effect on his direct reports, he told us, was heartening. The gentler and more encouraging he became, the more they responded. In the six months after his follow-up visit with us, his team's overall revenues increased by more than 15 percent—a period during which his company's overall performance was flat.

Twelve months after we first saw Roger, his career back on a fast track, he made another significant change in his schedule. One day a week, with permission from his boss, he began working at home. He felt convinced that he could use the time to escape the daily demands and to focus more attention on longer-range projects and issues that required more concentrated focus. At the same time, he was eager to be more involved with his children's daily lives. On the day that he worked at home, he took both of his children to school, picked them up in the afternoon and committed to stopping work by 5:00 p.m. The deepened connection with his girls was deeply satisfying, and he also found that the day at home was highly productive.

Skeptical and resistant as he was when he first came to see us, Roger was able to identify values and to create a vision that proved to be deeply compelling to him. They became both a high-octane fuel and a reliable touchstone when he was faced with difficult choices. His rituals were the means by which he lived out his vision, both at work and at home. "What amazes me most," Roger told us, "is that once my values became clear and I got the hang of building rituals, most of the changes I made weren't that hard. My life acquired a certain rhythm. I can feel how much my energy has rubbed off on the people in my life. My challenge now is just to feel the pulse and keep the beat."

RESOURCES

SUMMARY OF THE CORPORATE ATHLETE FULL-ENGAGEMENT TRAINING SYSTEM

1. **Objective:** Perform in the storm.

   • Build the necessary capacity to sustain high performance in the face of increasing demand.

2. **Central conclusion:** Energy is the fundamental currency of high performance.

   • Capacity is a function of one's ability to expend and recover energy.

   • Every thought, feeling and action has an energy consequence.

   • Energy is the most important individual and organizational resource.

3. **Full engagement:** Optimal energy in the context of high performance.

   • Physically energized

- Emotionally connected

- Mentally focused

- Spiritually aligned

4. **Full engagement is a consequence of the skillful management of energy in all dimensions.**

5. **Full engagement principles:**

   - Managing energy, not time, is the key to high performance.

   - Full engagement requires drawing on four separate but related dimensions of energy: physical, emotional, mental and spiritual.

   - Because energy capacity diminishes with both overuse and underuse, we must learn to balance energy expenditure with intermittent energy renewal.

   - To build capacity, we must push beyond our normal limits, training in the same systematic way that elite athletes do.

   - Positive energy rituals—highly specific routines for managing energy—are the key to full engagement and sustained high performance.

6. Full engagement requires drawing on four separate but related sources of energy:

- Physical capacity is reflected in one's ability to expend and recover energy at the physical level.

- Emotional capacity is reflected in one's ability to expend and recover energy at the emotional level.

- Mental capacity is reflected in one's ability to expend and recover energy at the mental level.

- Spiritual capacity is reflected in one's ability to expend and recover energy at the spiritual level.

- The most fundamental source of energy is physical. The most significant is spiritual.

7. Four sources of energy:

- Physical capacity is defined by quantity of energy.

- Emotional capacity is defined by quality of energy.

- Mental capacity is defined by focus of energy.

- Spiritual capacity is defined by force of energy.

8. **Measuring energy:**

   - The quantity of available energy is measured in terms of volume (low to high).

   - The quality of available energy is measured in terms of unpleasant (negative) to pleasant (positive).

   - The focus of available energy is measured in terms of broad to narrow and external to internal.

   - The force of available energy is measured in terms of self to others, external to internal and negative to positive.

9. **Optimal performance requires:**

   - Greatest quantity of energy

   - Highest quality of energy

   - Clearest focus of energy

   - Maximum force of energy

10. **Barriers to full engagement:** Negative habits that block, distort, waste, diminish, deplete and contaminate stored energy.

11. **The Full-Engagement Training System:** Removes barriers by establishing strategic positive energy rituals that insure sufficient capacity in all dimensions.

12. **Positive energy rituals support effective energy management.**

   • Skillful energy management requires summoning the appropriate quantity, quality, direction and force of energy.

13. **Lifelong energy objective:** To burn as brightly as possible for as long as possible in the service of what really matters.

   • Strongest possible physical pulse.

   • Strongest possible emotional pulse.

   • Strongest possible mental pulse.

   • Strongest possible spiritual pulse.

14. **Chronological age is fixed. Biological age can be modified with training.**

   • Biological age (reflected in performance capacity) is determined by one's ability to effectively expend and recover energy.

15. **Full engagement requires periodic strategic recovery.**

   • The energy that serves full engagement is renewed and stored during periods of strategic recovery (disengagement).

16. **The rhythmic movement between energy expenditure and energy recovery is called oscillation.**

- Oscillation refers to the optimal cycle of work/rest intervals.

- Chronic stress without recovery and chronic recovery without stress both serve to reduce capacity.

- In sport, these conditions are referred to as overtraining and undertraining.

17. **The opposite of oscillation is linearity.**

- Linearity is excessive stress without recovery or excessive recovery with insufficient stress.

- High-pressure situations generate powerful forces of linearity.

18. **Sustained high performance is best served by assuming the mentality of a sprinter not a marathoner.**

- Over the span of a thirty- to forty-year career, performance is optimized by scheduling work into 90- to 120-minute periods of intensive effort followed by shorter periods of recovery and renewal.

19. **Most of us are undertrained physically and spiritually (not enough stress) and overtrained mentally and emotionally (not enough recovery).**

20. **Interval (cyclical) exercise is far superior to steady-state (noncyclical) exercise in terms of enhancing energy-management skills.**

21. **Energy in the human system is multi dimensional.**

    - A dynamic relationship exists between physical, emotional, mental and spiritual energy.

    - Changes in any one dimension of energy affect all dimensions.

22. **Energy capacities follow developmental lines.**

    - First level of development is physical.

    - Second level of development is emotional/ social.

    - Third level of development is cognitive/ mental.

    - Fourth level of development is moral/spirit- ual.

23. **Each of the four dimensions follows its own developmental stages:** (E.g., emotional development, cognitive development, moral development.)

24. The Full Engagement training system begins spiritually with a connection to purpose.

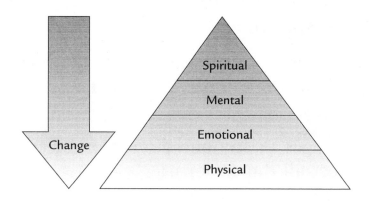

25. High positive energy is the fuel for high performance.

- High positive energy flows from the perception of opportunity, adventure and challenge (approach). Negative energy is precipated by the perception of threat, danger and fears about survival (avoidance).

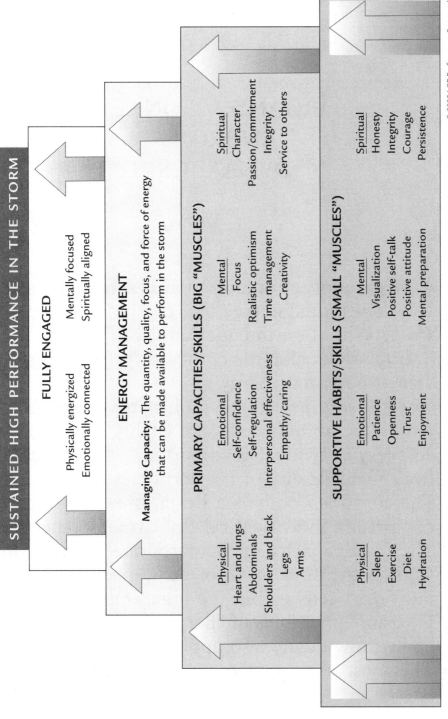

SUSTAINED HIGH PERFORMANCE IN THE STORM

FULLY ENGAGED

Physically energized   Mentally focused
Emotionally connected   Spiritually aligned

ENERGY MANAGEMENT

Managing Capacity: The quantity, quality, focus, and force of energy
that can be made available to perform in the storm

PRIMARY CAPACITIES/SKILLS (BIG "MUSCLES")

Physical	Emotional	Mental	Spiritual
Heart and lungs	Self-confidence	Focus	Character
Abdominals	Self-regulation	Realistic optimism	Passion/commitment
Shoulders and back	Interpersonal effectiveness	Time management	Integrity
Legs	Empathy/caring	Creativity	Service to others
Arms			

SUPPORTIVE HABITS/SKILLS (SMALL "MUSCLES")

Physical	Emotional	Mental	Spiritual
Sleep	Patience	Visualization	Honesty
Exercise	Openness	Positive self-talk	Integrity
Diet	Trust	Positive attitude	Courage
Hydration	Enjoyment	Mental preparation	Persistence

ORGANIZATIONAL ENERGY DYNAMICS

- A corporation or organization is simply a reservoir of potential energy that can be recruited in the service of an intended mission.
- Every individual in the corporate body is a reservoir of potential energy.
- Just as every cell in the human body is important to the overall health and vitality of the body, so every individual is important to the overall health and vitality of the corporate body.
- The corporate body is a living, breathing entity comprising individual cells of dynamic energy.
- The total capacity of the corporate body to do work is the sum of all of the capacities of the individual cells within the organization.
- The same principles of energy management that apply individually also apply organizationally.
- The most important organizational resource is energy.

- In order for an organization to optimize its potential, four separate but related forms of energy must be recruited in the service of the corporate mission: physical, emotional, mental and spiritual.
- Because energy in the corporate body is depleted from use, organizational energy expenditure must be balanced with energy recovery.
- Organizational energy capacity increases as individuals increase their collective capacity.
- A shared sense of corporate purpose, grounded in universal values, is the highest octane source of fuel for organizational action.
- The foundation of energy mobilization in the corporate body is physical. The quality of fitness, diet, sleep, rest and hydration among individuals plays a foundational role in determining overall organizational capacity.
- The corporate body has a strong or a weak physical pulse which reflects its capacity for rhythmically expending and recovering energy.
- The corporate body has a strong or weak emotional pulse which reflects its capacity for caring, compassion, confidence, enjoyment, and challenge.
- The corporate body has a strong or weak mental pulse which reflects its capacity for good decision making, logical thinking, clear focus and creativity.
- The corporate body has a strong or weak spiritual pulse reflecting its capacity for honesty, integrity, commitment and conviction.

- Leaders are the stewards of organizational energy. They recruit, direct, channel, renew, focus and invest energy from all the individual cells in the service of the corporate mission.
- Great leaders are experts in mobilizing and focusing all of the energy resources in the corporate body in the service of the corporate mission.
- Great leaders recognize that high positive energy is the fuel for high performance. Every aspect of their leadership clearly reflects this understanding.
- The energy of each individual cell in the corporate body must be actively recruited. This requires aligning individual and organizational purpose.
- Alignment drives performance. Lack of alignment significantly restricts the quantity, quality, direction and force of available energy.

MOST IMPORTANT PHYSICAL ENERGY MANAGEMENT STRATEGIES

1. Go to bed early and wake up early

2. Go to sleep and wake up consistently at the same times

3. Eat five to six small meals daily

4. Eat breakfast every day

5. Eat a balanced, healthy diet

6. Minimize simple sugars

7. Drink 48 to 64 ounces of water daily

8. Take breaks every ninety minutes during work

9. Get some physical activity daily

10. Do at least two cardiovascular interval work outs and two strength training workouts a week

GLYCEMIC INDEX EXAMPLES

Low	Moderate	High
Almonds	Apricots	Bagels
Apples	Bananas	Baked potatoes
Beans	Bean soups	Breads—some
Cabbage	Beets	Cakes
Cashews	Berries	Candy
Cherries	Biscuits	Carrots
Chicken	Breads—some	Cereals—many
Cottage cheese	Canned fruits	Cookies
Dried apricots	Cantelopes	Corn chips
Eggs	Cereal bars	Cupcakes

Grapefruits	Cereals—many	Dates, dried
Green vegetables	Chocolate	Donuts
Lentils	Corn	French fries
Milk	Couscous	Graham crackers
Mozzarella cheese	Crackers—most	Mashed potatoes
Nutrition bars—most	Croissants	Melba toast
Nutrition shakes	Fruit cocktail	Pretzels
Oranges	Granola	Pumpkin
Peaches	Grapes	Raisins
Peanut butter	Honey	Rice cakes
Peanuts	Ice cream	Saltine crackers
Pears	Juices	Sodas
Pecans	Kiwi	Sports drinks
Pistachios	Lentil soups	Tapioca pudding
Plums	Mangos	Vanilla wafers
Prunes	Muffins	Waffles

Pumpkin seeds	Oatmeal	Watermelon
Soy milk	Orange juice	
Split peas	Pasta	
Sunflower seeds	Pastries	
Tomato soup	Pea soups	
Tomatoes	Pineapple	
Tuna	Popcorn	
Turkey	Potato chips	
Walnuts	Raisins	
Yogurt (plain)	Rice	
	Sugar Sweet potatoes	

THE Corporate® ATHLETE

Personal Development Plan

Name: *Roger B.*

Date: *March 30, 2000*

VISION WORKSHEET

My deepest values:

1. Family
2. Respect & kindness toward others
3. Excellence
4. Integrity
5. Health

My strengths:

1. Loyalty
2. Organization
3. Focus
4. Ethical/Values-driven
5. Honesty

Jumping ahead to the end of your life, what are the three most important lessons you have learned and why are they so critical?

1. Marry someone you love and respect and always make your family your highest priority.

2. Work hard, keep your standards high, and never settle for anything less than you are capable of achieving.

3. Treat other people with respect and kindness.

Think of someone that you deeply respect. Describe the three qualities that you most admire in this person.
My father

1. His dignity

2. His gentleness

3. His integrity regardless of the challenges he faced

Who are you at your best?

Caring, passionate, hard-working, funny and someone you can count on

What is the one sentence inscription you would like to see on your tombstone that captures who you really were in your life?

He cared. And he never stopped trying to give more of himself to others.

322

Write your vision statement(s) in the present tense. It should be both practical and deeply inspirational.

My Personal Vision (reflecting my deepest values):

My highest priority in life is my wife and children. When we are together, I am committed to giving them all of my energy and attention. To make that possible, I must also take care of myself physically.

_____

_____

_____

_____

My Work/Career Vision (reflecting my personal vision and values):

At work, I hold myself to a high standard of excellence. As a leader, I model each of my primary values—most of all kindness, concern for others and integrity. I make others feel cared for and confident that they can count on me to live up to my commitments. Whatever I do, I do wholeheartedly.

_____

_____

_____

_____

323

BARRIERS WORKSHEET

My Top Work-Related Performance Barriers	Energy/Performance Consequences
1. Low energy	Poor performance, relationships lack depth, compromised happiness.
2. Impatience	Promotes negative energy in myself and others. Leads to insecurity and low confidence in others and makes me tense and uptight.
3. Negative thinker	I end up in high negative and low negative energy states constantly at work and home.
4. Relationships lack depth	Compromises leadership and connections to family and friends.
5. Lack of passion	Undermines persistence and commitment. Life has little color—everything is gray. Can't generate any real excitement or force.

324

ACTION & DEVELOPMENT PLAN FOR FULL ENGAGEMENT

Ritual-Building Strategy

Targeted Muscle(s): Heart & lungs, upper & lower body

Performance Barrier: Low energy

Value(s) driving change: Family

Expected performance consequence: Higher productivity, fewer errors, better decisions

Positive Energy Rituals Supporting the Targeted Change:	Launch Date					
1. Exercise: Work out 3 times/week—Tuesdays & Fridays at 1:00 pm and Saturdays at 10:00 am (emphasis on interval training).	4/1					
2. Break every 90 minutes during work.	4/1					
3. Take snacks when traveling. Eat and drink every 90 minutes to 2 hours on the road.	5/1					
4. Leave office by 5:30 p.m. 2 days per week.	6/1					

ACTION & DEVELOPMENT PLAN FOR FULL ENGAGEMENT

Ritual-Building Strategy

Targeted Muscle(s): Patience

Performance Barrier: Impatience

Value(s) driving change: Respect and kindness toward others

Expected performance consequence: More positive energy for myself and for those around me. More fully engaged.

Positive Energy Rituals Supporting the Targeted Change:	Launch Date
1. 6:30 a.m. every morning read my vision statement.	4/1
2. Break every 90 minutes during work.	4/1
3. Take snacks when traveling. Eat and drink every 90 minutes to 2 hours on the road.	5/1
4. Specific "emergency" ritual whenever I start feeling impatient or agitated.	4/1

ACTION & DEVELOPMENT PLAN FOR FULL ENGAGEMENT

Ritual-Building Strategy

Targeted Muscle(s): Realistic optimism

Performance Barrier: Negative thinking

Value(s) driving change: Integrity, excellence

Expected performance consequence: Higher productivity due to more positive energy and focus

Positive Energy Rituals Supporting the Targeted Change:	Launch Date
1. Preparation on way to work—review day's activities and rehearse positive framing.	4/1
2. Break every 90 minutes during work.	4/1
3. Take snacks when traveling. Eat and drink every 90 minutes to 2 hours on the road.	5/1
4. Specific "emergency" ritual whenever I start feeling impatient or agitated.	4/1

ACTION & DEVELOPMENT PLAN FOR FULL ENGAGEMENT

Ritual-Building Strategy

Targeted Muscle(s): Caring, compassion, friendship

Performance Barrier: Relationships lack depth

Value(s) driving change: Family, integrity, respect and kindness toward others

Expected performance consequence: Better communication with team members, family; more positive energy

Positive Energy Rituals Supporting the Targeted Change:	Launch Date
1. On commute home—call to someone I care about.	5/1
2. Morning note to children.	5/1
3. Breakfast at home with Rachel [wife].	5/1
4. Brunch with girls on Sunday afternoon.	6/1
5. Lunch with direct report each week.	6/1
6. Pick up children at school on the day I work from home.	5/1

ACTION & DEVELOPMENT PLAN FOR FULL ENGAGEMENT

Ritual-Building Strategy

Targeted Muscle(s): Passion, conviction

Performance Barrier: Lacking passion

Value(s) driving change: Family, integrity

Expected performance consequence: Greater persistence and resilience

Positive Energy Rituals Supporting the Targeted Change:

		Launch Date
1.	Preparation on way to work—review day's activities and rehearse positive framing.	4/1
2.	Vision statement on screensaver.	4/1

ACCOUNTABILITY LOG

Name: _____ ROGER B. _____ Week of: _____

Directions: Rate yourself daily in each of these areas using the 5–1 scale (5 = very successful, 1 = not successful). Add any notes on behavior, chronic obstacles, "a-ha's," etc. Also record times and effects wherever appropriate.

Rituals	Sun	Mon	Tue	Wed	Thu	Fri	Sat	Notes
Visit values 1st thing in A.M.								
Breakfast at home w/ Rachel								
Brunch w/ girls on Sunday								
Morning note to children								
Review day's activities								
Eat & drink every 90 min.–2 hrs.								
Break every 90 min. at work								
Lunch w/ direct report weekly								
Emergency patience rituals								
Call loved ones on way home								
Leave office by 5:30—2x/wk								
Interval workout 3x/wk								
Pick up children from school on day home								

Accomplishments: _____

The Corporate ATHLETE®

Personal Development Plan

Name: _____

Date: _____

VISION WORKSHEET

My deepest values:

1. _____
2. _____
3. _____
4. _____
5. _____

My strengths:

1. _____
2. _____
3. _____
4. _____
5. _____

Jumping ahead to the end of your life, what are the three most important lessons you have learned and why are they so critical?

1. _____
2. _____
3. _____

Think of someone that you deeply respect. Describe the three qualities that you most admire in this person.

1. _____
2. _____
3. _____

Who are you at your best?

_____

What is the one sentence inscription you would like to see on your tombstone that captures who you really were in your life?

_____

Write your vision statement(s) in the present tense. It should be both practical and deeply inspirational.

My Personal Vision (reflecting my deepest values):

_____

_____

_____

_____

_____

_____

_____

My Work/Career Vision (reflecting my personal vision and values):

_____

_____

_____

_____

_____

_____

333

BARRIERS WORKSHEET

My Top Work-Related Performance Barriers	Energy/Performance Consequences

ACTION & DEVELOPMENT PLAN FOR FULL ENGAGEMENT

Ritual-Building Strategy

Targeted Muscle(s):

Performance Barrier:

Value(s) driving change:

Expected performance consequence:

Positive Energy Rituals Supporting the Targeted Change:	Launch Date

ACCOUNTABILITY LOG

Name: _____   Week of: _____

Directions: Rate yourself daily in each of these areas using the 5–1 scale (5 = very successful, 1 = not successful). Add any notes on behavior, chronic obstacles, "a-ha's," etc. Also record times and effects wherever appropriate.

Rituals	Sun	Mon	Tue	Wed	Thu	Fri	Sat	Notes

Accomplishments: _____

ACKNOWLEDGMENTS

We must first acknowledge one another. Both of us have spent our adult lives as seekers. Jim's early work focused on the source of human capacity—what makes it possible for some people to perform at the highest levels even under extraordinary pressure. Tony's passion was trying to understand the nature of wisdom—what constitutes a satisfying, productive and well-lived life.

Friends for more than a decade, the two of us began working together five years ago to see if the sum of our ideas might be greater than the parts. It was a rich and exciting collaboration from the first day. For the next three years, we began nearly every morning at 6:30 a.m. by talking for as much as two hours, developing the model and change process that we use with our clients and which became the basis for this book.

337

Jim's work began from the bottom up, focused on behavior and performance as the crucible upon which to measure success. Tony's work came from the top down, focused on meaning and purpose as the most powerful sources of direction and motivation. Together, we developed an integrated, multidimensional model of high performance and full engagement. The skillful management of energy proved to be the common denominator. These ideas are a work-in-progress, which is good news for our partnership. For both of us, this has been the most rewarding experience in our professional lives—a source of shared passion, unending challenge and great joy.

This book is wholly our responsibility, but it is the product of many minds. Jack Groppel came up with the term Corporate Athlete twenty years ago, and he has been our partner, comrade, sounding board and supporter all through this process. No one articulates the concepts of the Corporate Athlete better than he does. Steve Dolan brought us discipline and a relentless focus on improving our process at all levels.

For their terrific creative contributions, we are especially indebted to our colleagues at LGE Performance Systems: Mark Anshel, Raquel Crocker, George Kyriazis, Marti Ludwig, Catherine McCarthy, Brian Wallace and Garth Weiss. Will Marre read what we thought was the final draft of this manuscript and had a series of brilliant insights about how to reorganize it. They proved to be invaluable. Chris Osorio is our newest partner, and he is already bringing an exceptional array of skills to the table.

Our entire staff at LGE is first rate. We must give special thanks to two of them. Renate Gaisser has been at LGE since its inception, and without her passion, dedication and resourcefulness, we would not have survived the tough times. Our assistant, Becky Hoholski, has lived through literally dozens of iterations of these ideas during the past three years. She is patient, committed, resilient and terrific at what she does. It is a pleasure to work with her every day.

We are indebted to many great thinkers from the past, and to a series of contemporaries whose work deeply influenced our own. Most notably, we have spent many hours discussing these ideas with Robert Kegan and Lisa Lahey, whose insights into what prevents people from making change that endures are both brilliant and unique. We have also benefited from the ideas and the enthusiasm of Richard Boyatzis, whose model of change and supportive research has been inspirational to us. In attempting to build an integrated model of full engagement, we also derived great value from the work of Mihaly Csikszentmihalyi, Dan Goleman, Jim Collins, Stephen Covey, David Myers, Martin Moore-Ede, Ernest Rossi and Martin Seligman. The compendium of essays in Connie Zweig and Jeremiah Abrams' *Meeting the Shadow* gather many great thinkers on the subject of why we so resist looking at the truth and the costs we incur as a result.

We are also deeply indebted to our loyal and supportive clients who have been willing to extend themselves in order to bring our program to their organizations. We are especially grateful to Bruce Brereton, Marcy Coen Smith, Robert DeFazio and Lori Kramer at Salomon Smith Barney, as well as to Rob Knapp at Merrill Lynch, Charles Cohen at Bencobental, Scott Miller and Ty Helms at Hyatt, Pat Crull at McDonald's, Dan Brestle and Phebe Farrow Port at Estée Lauder, Steve Reinemund at Pepsico and Peter Scaturro at Citigroup.

Our agent, Alice Martel, was absolutely passionate about this project from the first day that we presented the ideas to her in a very primitive form. She managed to get many other people excited, and since then has read every draft of the manuscript, dogged every detail and promoted the book at every opportunity. We treasure her.

Fred Hills at The Free Press was also fiercely passionate about the potential for this book from the first time he read our outline. He has been both our editor and our advocate throughout this process. We are also appreciative to all of the others at The Free Press who have worked hard to make this book happen including Martha Levin, Dominick Anfuso, Suzanne Donahue, Carissa Hays and Kelly Gionti. And especially to Carolyn Reidy, whose initial enthusiasm compelled us to bring this book to Simon & Schuster.

A special thanks Vicky and Bob Zoellner for their unwavering support and their belief in the vision from day one; to Gordon Uehling for helping to bring the dream to life; and to so many who have helped us along the way: Jeff Balash, Brad Blum, Dan Brestle, Dick Fox, Joe Torrez, John Gilbank, Fred Kiel, Mike Lawson, Peter Moore, Mark Pacala, Jeff Sklar and Kathryn Williams.

JIM'S ACKNOWLEDGMENTS

I want to thank to all of the athletes who have touched my life and formed the basis of my thinking about capacity and high performance, most importantly Jim Courier, Tom Gullikson, Dan Jansen and Mike Richter.

I also wish to acknowledge the contributions made by countless sport and exercise psychology researchers, most especially Diane Gill, Daniel Gould, Robert Singer and Wesley Sime.

I am also deeply appreciative of Howard Brody, Todd Ellenbecker, Randy Gerber, Ryan Macaulay, Doug MacCurdy, Mark and Betsy McCormack, Rob Palumbo, Tore and Eddie Resavage, Paul Roetert, Stan Smith, Kathy Toon, Dennis and Pat Van der Meer, and Amy Wishingrad.

Thanks to my brother Tom and sister Jane (Sister Mary Margaret Loehr) whose lives fully embody what this book is all about. To Renate for her unfailing love, support and belief through every storm. Finally, to my three sons, Mike, Pat and

Jeff, who are the core of meaning in my life and have always been my greatest teachers. Above all, they are an unending source of my happiness and my passion for life.

TONY'S ACKNOWLEDGMENTS

I want to thank all of the people in my life who have endured my obsession with these ideas, contributed to my thinking and helped to keep me (relatively) balanced and humble:

I reserve a special place for my "little brother" Al Edmond, who has taught me a great deal about courage, survival and hope. Nathan Schwartz-Salant has been a huge influence in my life. He has helped me to navigate through nearly every crisis I've faced during the past decade and more. I am especially touched that Jane Eisen, my friend since we were in diapers, went through our program, took it on as a cause and persuaded Brown University Medical School to incorporate it into the training of medical students. Karen Page has been an extraordinary friend and advocate and, with her peerless networking skills, has put me in front of more high-level audiences than I can count. I have enjoyed discussing and debating the ideas in this book with Richard Boyatzis, Marcus Buckingham, and for many years with Ken Wilber. I'm also appreciative to Cassie Arnold, Andrew Dornenburg, Michael Fiori, Marc Gunther, Laura Lau, Doug Lind, Kathy Reilly,

Paul Rumeley, James O. Schwartz, Rich Simon, Fred Studier and Steven and Nancy Weinstock.

Finally, of course, there is my family. My daughters, Kate and Emily, have grown up into very different but equally wonderful young women. What they share is integrity, passion, independence and very big hearts. They make me proud every day, and they also make me very happy.

I can't possibly do justice to Deborah in a few words—or for that matter with any words. She has been my partner every step of the way. We have grown up together, and it has been an incredible, challenging, wonderful journey. When I wrote Deborah an acknowledgment in my last book, I ended it by saying "After eighteen years, she is—more than ever—the love of my life." That is more true than ever after twenty-five years. I fully expect it to be even truer twenty-five years from now.

NOTES

One Fully Engaged

Less than 30 percent: Private correspondence with Marcus Buckingham.

Two The Disengaged Life of Roger B.

When he came: Roger B. is an actual client. As with other clients described in the book, we have changed his name and certain identifying details. In some cases, the clients we describe are composites.

Three The Pulse of High Performance

In the 1970s: Ernest Rossi, *The 20-Minute Break* (Los Angeles: Tarcher, 1991), p. viii.
I was blessed: Jack Nicklaus, "My Strongest Weapon" *Golf*, December 1993, pp. 47–48.

At the heart of: Martin Moore-Ede, *The Twenty-Four-Hour Society* (Reading, Mass.: Addison-Wesley, 1993), p. 6.

Consider the way that: Tony Schwartz, "Going Postal" *New York Magazine*, July 19, 1999, p. 34.

A study conducted: Ibid., p. 35

Moore-Ede calls this: Moore-Ede, p. 204.

As Wayne Muller puts it: Wayne Muller, *Sabbath* (New York: Bantam, 1999), p. 2.

Take Dick Wolf: Tony Schwartz, "Acceleration Syndrome: How Life Got Much, Much Too Fast," *Vanity Fair*, October 1988, p. 180.

For Mark Ethridge: Ibid., p. 148.

Workaholism is an obsessive: Bryan Robinson, *Chained to the Desk* (New York: New York University Press, 1998), pp. 6–7.

Researchers have found: Ibid., p. 149.

The first case of karoshi: Katsuo Nishiyama and Jeffrey V. Johnson. *Karoshi—Death from Overwork: Occupational Health Consequences of the Japanese Production Management.* Sixth Draft for International Journal of Health Services, February 4, 1997, Workhealth.org. 1–15.

The number of: Ibid.

One case study: Ibid.

Nancy Woodhull was: Schwartz, "Acceleration Syndrome," p. 180.

The same paradoxical: Mihaly Csikszentmihalyi, *Flow* (New York: Simon & Schuster, 1989), p. 3.

Four Physical Energy

In one study: Rossi, *The 20-Minute Break*, p. 122.

In a second study: Proceedings of the 10th International Congress on Nutrition.

Thirty-five percent: Gina Kolata, "Asking if Obesity Is a Disease or Just a Symptom," *New York Times*, April 16, 2002, p. D5.

Even small amounts: Moore-Ede, *The Twenty-Four-Hour Society*, pp. 58–59.

Numerous studies: Ibid., p. 67

On a broader scale: Ibid., p. 6.

Three years after Libby: Ibid., pp. 102–103.

In 2002, the national: Lawrence K. Altman and Denise Grady, "Hospital Accreditor will strictly limit hours of residents," *New York Times*, June 13, 2002, p. A1.

According to: Moore-Ede, *The Twenty-Four-Hour Society*, p. 103.

The cost of implementing: Ibid.

The documented vulnerability: Rossi, *The 20-Minute Break*, p. 112.

NASA's Fatigue Counter Measures: Susan Brink, "Sleepless Society," *U.S. News & World Report*, October 16, 2000, pp. 62–72; "A Quick Power Nap's Benefits," *New York Times*, May 28, 2002, p. F6.

You must sleep some time: Rossi, *The 20-Minute Break*, p. 21.

The link between: (DuPont) *American Journal of Health Promotion*, Kenneth R. Pelletier, editor,

March/April 1991; (A study in) Hans Sjoberg, Ergonomics, 1983; (In a study of) Robert J. Brosmer, Deborah L. Waldron, *Health and High Performance*, 1991; (*The Canadian*) Dennis Thompson, Personnel, March 1990; (*At Union Pacific*) Joe Leutzinger, Daniel Blanke, *Health Values*, September/October, 1991; (*General Motors found*) *Commercial Magazine*, October 1998; (*The Coors Brewing*) *This Is Corporate Wellness and Its Bottom Line Impact*, Wellness Council of America, 1991.

On average, we lose: Miriam Nelson, *Strong Women Stay Young* (New York: Bantam, 1997), p. 22.

A controlled study: Ibid., p. 11.

By the age of ninety: Ibid., p. 44.

Rigorous training improves: Dr. C. A. Morgan III and Major Gary Hazlett, "Assessment of Humans Experiencing Uncontrollable Stress: The SERE Course," *Special Warfare*, Summer 2000, p. 6.

Five   Emotional Energy

From our perspective: In his book *Working with Emotional Intelligence*, Daniel Goleman includes motivation as a key emotional intelligence competence. We believe that the highest form of motivation comes from a connection to deeply held values and a strong sense of purpose—something we call spiritual. Goleman also identifies self-awareness as a key emotional competence. We believe that self-awareness is a prerequisite to effectiveness in the physical, mental and spiritual dimensions as well, and is not uniquely characteristic of emotional intelligence.

Upon analysis: David Snowdon, *Aging with Grace* (New York: Bantam, 2001), p. 115.

Nuns with the highest. Ibid., p. 194.

This is consistent: Ibid., p. 82.

"I try not to": Ibid., p. 196.

"My shtick, of course": John McEnroe, *You Cannot Be Serious.* (New York: Putnam, 2002), p. 178

"I wasted too much energy": Ibid., p. 181

After interviewing a large: Marcus Buckingham and Curt Coffman, *First Break All the Rules* (New York: Simon & Schuster, 2000), p. 32.

For the most part: Csikszentmihalyi, *Flow*, pp. 30–169.

Gallup found: Buckingham and Coffman, *First Break All the Rules*, pp. 28–29.

Alan decided. For a highly structured and effective approach to increasing listening skills, we recommend Harville Hendrix's "Intentional Dialogue," which he developed for couples and describes in *Keeping the Love You Find* (New York Pocket Books, 1993).

To be fully engaged.: Michael Murphy, *The Future of the Body* (Los Angeles: Tarcher, 1992), pp. 558–559.

We also need: Sandra L. Schneider. "In Search of Realistic Optimism," *American Psychologist* 56, 3 (March 2001): 250–263.

When scores were: Martin E. P. Seligman, *Learned Optimism* (New York: Knopf, 1990), pp. 99–102.

In his provocative book: Michael J. Gelb, *How to Think Like Leonardo da Vinci* (New York: Dell, 1998), p. 160.

"It is a very good plan": Ibid., p. 158.

In her books: Betty Edwards: *Drawing on the Right Side of the Brain* (Los Angeles: Tarcher, 1989), and *Drawing on the Artist Within* (New York: Fireside, 1986).

At Baylor College: Jean Carper, *Your Miracle Brain* (New York: HarperCollins, 2000), p. 35.

As neurologist Richard: Richard Restak, *Mozart's Brain and the Fighter Pilot* (New York: Harmony Books, 2000), p. 41.

Exercise is also believed: Tara Parker-Pope, "Help Combat Senility: Learn a Language, Read a Good Book," *Wall Street Journal*, November 23, 2001, p. 31.

In the absence of downtime: Restak, *Mozart's Brain and the Fighter Pilot*, p. 5.

Every time you learn: Parker-Pope, "Help Combat Senility," p. 31.

Stephen Covey captures: Stephen Covey, *The 7 Habits of Highly Effective People* (New York: Simon & Schuster, 1989), p. 151.

Seven Spiritual Energy

According to Heidi: Diana B. Henriques, "Cantor Survivors on a Mission," *New York Times*, November 2, 2002, p. D1.

Woe to him who saw. Victor E. Frankl, *Man's Search for Meaning* (New York: Washington Square Press, 1985), p. 98.

Mental health is: Ibid., p. 127.

The truth is that: Lance Armstrong, *It's Not About the Bike* (New York: Putnam, 2000), pp. 265, 273.

Eight Defining Purpose

You can work long hours: Joanne Ciulla, *The Working Life* (New York: Times Books, 2000), p. 255.

As Viktor Frankl puts it: Frankl, *Man's Search for Meaning*, p. 131.

A study conducted by: Richard M. Ryan and Edward L. Deci, "Self-Determination Theory and the Facilitation of Intrinsic Motivation, Social Development, and Well-Being," *American Psychologist* 55, 1 (January 2000): 68–78.

While money serves: David G. Myers, *The Pursuit of Happiness* (New York: Avon Books, 1992), p. 41.

We humans need: Ibid., p. 43.

Extrinsic rewards have: E. L. Koestner and R. M. Ryan, "A meta-analytic review of experiments examining the effects of extrinsic rewards of intrinsic motivation," *Psychological Bulletin* 125 (1999): 627–668.

Work makes life better: Joan B. Ciulla, *The Working Life* (New York: Times Books, 2000), pp. 225–226.

Nine   Face the Truth

The range of what: Connie Zweig and Jeremiah Abrams, *Meeting the Shadow: The Hidden Power of the Dark Side of Human Nature* (Los Angeles: Tarcher/Putnam, 1990), p. xix.

When Lauren Manning: *New York Times*, December 12, 2001, p. B1.

Every form of addiction: Zweig and Abrams, *Meeting the Shadow*, p. 171.

We often see anger: Ibid., p. 178.

In Buddhism, the form: Joseph Goldstein and Jack Kornfield, *Seeking the Heart of Wisdom* (Boston: Shambhala, 1993), p. 94.

The central defect: Zweig and Abrams, *Meeting the Shadow*, p. 176.

It is not until we: Ibid., p. 16.

When our explanatory beliefs: Seligman, Learned Optimism, p. 259.

In his book: Jim Collins, *Good to Great* (New York: HarperBusiness, 2001), pp. 12–13.

Ask someone to give: Zweig and Abrams, *Meeting the Shadow*, p. 14.

Ten Taking Action

A growing body: Roy Baumeister and K. L. Sommer, "Consciousness, free choice and automaticity," in *Advances in Social Cognition*, vol. X, ed. R. S. Myer, Jr. (Mahwah, N.J.: Erlbaum), 75–81; John A. Bargh and Tanya L. Chartrand. "The Unbearable Automaticity of Being." *American Psychologist* 54, 7 (July 1999): 462–479.

Families who sit down: Evan Imber-Black and Janine Roberts, *Rituals for Our Times* (New York: Harper Perennial, 1992), p. 45.

The precise opposite: A. N. Whitehead, *An Introduction to Mathematics* (New York: Holt, 1911).

Each time that Lendl: Tony Schwartz, "Obsession: Ivan Lendl's Lonely Quest for Perfection," *New York Magazine*, June 26, 1989, p. 41.

A broad and persuasive: Mark Muraven and Roy F. Baumeister, "Self-Regulation and Depletion of Limited Resources: Does Self Control Resemble a Muscle?" *Psychological Bulletin* 126, 2 (2000): 240.

In one study: Peter M. Gollwitzer. "Implementation Intentions," *American Psychologist* 54, 7 (July 1999): 493–503.

At all times the focus: Bill Walsh, *Finding the Winning Edge* (Champaign, Ill.: Sports Publishing, 1998), p. 16.

I have found that: "Don't Burn Out!" *Fast Company*, May 2000, p. 106.

It's great to know: Ibid., p. 129.

BIBLIOGRAPHY

Armstrong, Lance. *It's Not About the Bike*. New York: Putnam, 2000.

Assagioli, Roberto, M.D. *Psychosynthesis*. New York: Penguin, 1976.

Buckingham, Marcus, and Curt Coffman. *First Break All the Rules*. New York: Simon & Schuster, 1999.

Buckingham, Marcus, and Donald O. Clifton. *Now, Discover Your Strengths*. New York: Simon & Schuster, 2001.

Cameron, Julia. *The Artist's Way*. New York: Tarcher/Putnam, 1992.

Campbell, Joseph. *The Portable Jung*. New York: Penguin, 1971.

————, with Bill Moyers. *The Power of Myth*. New York: Anchor Books, 1988.

Carper, Jean. *Your Miracle Brain*. New York: HarperCollins, 2000.

353

Ciulla, Joanne B. *The Working Life*. New York: Times Books, 2000.

Collins, Jim C. *Good to Great*. New York: HarperBusiness, 2001.

———, and Jerry I. Porras. *Built to Last*. New York: HarperBusiness, 1994.

Coren, Stanley. *Sleep Thieves*. New York: Free Press, 1996.

Covey, Stephen R. *The 7 Habits of Highly Effective People*. New York: Simon & Schuster, 1989.

Csikszentmihalyi, Mihaly. *Flow*. New York: HarperPerennial, 1990.

Dalai Lama and Howard C. Cutler. *The Art of Happiness*. New York: Riverhead Books, 1998.

Edwards, Betty. *Drawing on the Artist Within*. New York: Fireside, 1986.

———. *Drawing on the Right Side of the Brain*. Los Angeles: Tarcher, 1989.

Epictetus. *The Art of Living*. New York: HarperCollins, 1995.

Evans, William J., and Gerald Secor Couzens. *Astrofit*. New York: Free Press, 2002.

Frankl, Viktor E. *Man's Search for Meaning*. New York: Washington Square Press, 1985.

Gelb, Michael. *How to Think Like Leonardo da Vinci*. New York: Dell, 1998.

Goldstein, Joseph. *Insight Meditation*. Boston: Shambhala, 1993.

Goldstein, Joseph, and Jack Kornfield. *Seeking the Heart of Wisdom*. Boston: Shambhala, 1987.

Goleman, Daniel. *Emotional Intelligence.* New York: Bantam, 1995.

———. *Vital Lies, Simple Truths: The Psychology of Self-Deception.* New York: Touchstone, 1986.

———. *Working with Emotional Intelligence.* New York: Bantam, 1998.

Groppel, Jack. *The Corporate Athlete.* New York: Wiley, 2000.

Imber-Black, Evan, and Janine Roberts. *Rituals for Our Times.* HarperPerennial, 1992.

Jung, Carl. *Modern Man in Search of a Soul.* New York: Harcourt Brace, 1936.

Kegan, Robert, and Lisa Laskow Lahey. *How the Way We Talk Can Change the Way We Work.* San Francisco: Jossey-Bass, 2001.

Kirkwood, Tom. *Time of Our Lives: The Science of Human Aging.* New York: Oxford University Press, 1999.

Leonard, George. *The Silent Pulse.* New York: E. P. Dutton, 1978.

LeShan, Lawrence. *How to Meditate.* New York: Bantam, 1974.

Loehr, James E. *The New Toughness Training for Sports.* New York: Plume, 1995.

———. *Toughness Training for Life.* New York: Dutton, 1993.

———. *Stress for Success.* New York: Times Business, 1997.

———, and Jeffrey A. Migdow. *Breathe In, Breathe Out.* New York: Villard Books, 1986.

Maslow, Abraham. *Toward a Psychology of Being.* Princeton, N.J.: Van Nostrand, 1962.

McEnroe, John. *You Cannot Be Serious.* New York: Putnam, 2002.

Moore-Ede, Martin. *The Twenty-Four-Hour Society.* Reading, Mass.: Addison-Wesley, 1993.

Muller, Wayne. *Sabbath.* New York: Bantam, 1999.

Murphy, Michael. *The Future of the Body.* Los Angeles: Tarcher, 1992.

Myers, David G. *The Pursuit of Happiness.* New York: Avon Books, 1992.

Nelson, Miriam E. *Strong Women Stay Young.* New York: Bantam, 1997.

Newberg, Andrew, Eugene D'Aquili and Vince Rause. *Why God Won't Go Away.* New York: Ballantine Books, 2001.

Proschaska, James O., John C. Norcross and Carlo C. Diclemente. *Changing for Good.* New York: Avon Books, 1994.

Restak, Richard. *Mozart's Brain and the Fighter Pilot.* New York: Harmony Books, 2001.

Robinson, Bryan W. *Chained to the Desk.* New York: New York University Press, 1998.

Roizen, Michael F. *Real Age.* New York: Cliff Street Books, 1999.

Rossi, Ernest Lawrence. *The 20-Minute Break.* Los Angeles: Tarcher, 1991.

Schwartz, Tony. *What Really Matters.* New York: Bantam, 1995.

Seligman, Martin E. P. *Learned Optimism.* New York: Knopf, 1990.

Snowdon, David. *Aging with Grace*. New York: Bantam, 2001.

Walsh, Bill. *Finding the Winning Edge*. Champaign, Ill.: Sports Publishing, 1998.

Wilber, Ken. *A Brief History of Everything*. Boston: Shambhala, 1996.

Zweig, Connie, and Jeremiah Abrams. *Meeting the Shadow: The Hidden Power of the Dark Side of Human Nature*. Los Angeles: Tarcher/ Putnam, 1990.

ABOUT THE AUTHORS

Jim Loehr, Ed.D., is the chairman and CEO of LGE Performance Systems and is recognized worldwide for his contributions to the field of performance psychology. He has worked with hundreds of world-class athletes, as well as with police departments, SWAT teams, emergency service workers and the FBI's elite Hostage Rescue team. Loehr cofounded LGE in 1993 to begin applying principles developed during his work with athletes to corporate executives. He has authored twelve books, including the best-selling *Stress for Success* and *Toughness Training for Sports*. He has also written numerous scientific articles and was for ten years a monthly columnist for *World Tennis* and *Tennis Magazine*.

Tony Schwartz is the president of LGE Performance Systems. Along with Jim Loehr, he developed the content and methodology for LGE's training programs, including the Corporate Athlete Executive Training. He is the co-author of three books, including the No. 1 bestselling *Art of the Deal* with Donald Trump (1989), *What Really Matters: Searching for Wisdom in America* (1996), and *Work in Progress* with Michael Eisner (1998). He has been a reporter for *The New York Times*, an associate editor for *Newsweek*, and a staff writer for *New York Magazine*. He has also contributed to *Esquire*, *Vanity Fair*, *The New Yorker*, *Gentlemen's Quarterly* and *Fast Company*, where for two years he wrote a monthly column titled "Life/Work."